VATCH'S **THAI KITCHEN**

VATCH'S **THAI KITCHEN**

Thai dishes to cook at home

Vatcharin Bhumichitr

Photography by Peter Cassidy

RYLAND
PETERS
& SMALL

LONDON NEW YORK

Dedication

To my friends

First published in the United States in 2005
by Ryland Peters & Small, Inc.
519 Broadway, 5th Floor
New York, NY 10012
www.rylandpeters.com

Senior Designer Steve Painter
Commissioning Editor Elsa Petersen-Schepelern
Editor Susan Stuck
Production Patricia Harrington
Art Director Gabriella Le Grazie
Publishing Director Alison Starling

Food Stylist Linda Tubby
Prop Stylist Róisín Nield
Indexer Hilary Bird

Text © Vatcharin Bhumichitr 2005
Design and photographs
© Ryland Peters & Small 2005

Library of Congress Cataloging-in-Publication Data

Vatcharin Bhumichitr.

Vatch's Thai kitchen : Thai dishes to cook at home /
Vatcharin Bhumichitr ; photography by Peter Cassidy.

p. cm.

Includes bibliographical references and index.

ISBN 10: 1-84172-808-X (alk. paper)
ISBN 13: 978-1-84172-808-7

1. Cookery, Thai. I. Title.

TX724.5.T5V39 2005

641.59593--dc22

2004024123

Printed and bound in China

Notes

• All spoon measurements are level unless otherwise stated.

• All herbs are fresh, unless specified otherwise.

• Eggs are large unless otherwise specified. Uncooked or
partially cooked eggs should not be served to the very old,
frail, young children, pregnant women, or those with
compromised immune systems.

• Most ingredients will be available in supermarkets. Others
are widely sold in Chinatown markets and Asian stores. To
order online or by mail order and for a list of speciality
outlets, please see page 142.

• Galangal is a popular ingredient in Thai spice pastes
and other dishes. It is widely available in markets selling
Southeast Asian produce. It can be successful frozen and
used straight from frozen. A common substitute in the West
is fresh ginger, though it has a totally different flavor and the
recipes will not taste the same.

(v) Dishes suitable for vegetarians.

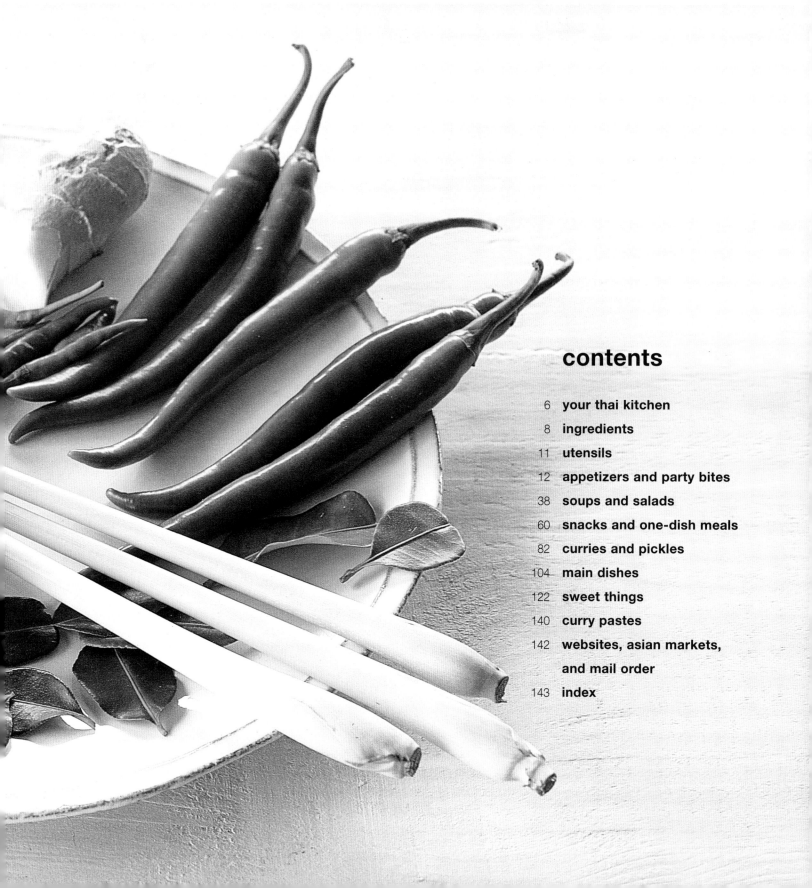

contents

YOUR THAI KITCHEN

It was dawn, and I was just waking after the first night in my new house in Ko Samui, Thailand. I remembered waking up as a child in my parents' house in Bangkok. The ground floor of the house was brick, painted a sun-bleached yellow, and the upper floor was timber. It was a big house with balconies on the upper floor: in the front they overlooked the garden, in the back they overlooked a courtyard, the maid's house, and the kitchen. This is the traditional layout for Thai houses with the kitchen in the back, separated from the house, sometimes linked by a covered walkway. I remember it as the source of the most wonderful smells and food.

My new house in Ko Samui has a similar layout, but it is built entirely of wood. The ground floor has shutters in the front and rear that fold back, so it can be completely open to the breeze. On that first night, I slept on the ground floor with the rear shutters open and when I woke I saw the back courtyard, then beyond the courtyard was the sea, and to the right an empty kitchen.

My first job and pleasure that day was to buy everything for my new kitchen. In this book, I will tell you all that you need to cook Thai food in a Western kitchen. Where I live, I am fortunate that I have to walk only 200 yards and I am in the local market that caters both to Buddhists and the local Muslim fishing community. I doubt that you will have such a selection of foods available to you, but in the following recipes I use ingredients that are generally available in Asian stores or large supermarkets. Nowadays, almost everything you need to cook authentic Thai food is readily available, and a list of websites and stores selling Thai ingredients and utensils appears on page 142.

ingredients

Cilantro *Pak chee*

Cilantro is also known as coriander leaf or Chinese parsley—it is, indeed, a member of the parsley family and much resembles Italian flat-leaf parsley. Like its relation, cilantro is generally used as a topping in Thailand, whole or chopped up and sprinkled on a finished dish, as much for the visual effect as the flavor.

Cilantro root is much used in Thailand—some dishes require a great many roots and this often creates a problem in the West, where suppliers often chop off the root. One solution is to persuade your produce store to get some uncut cilantro or for you to look for any bunches with one or two roots still surviving. Alternatively, grow your own. Cut off the roots with about ⅛ inch of the stalk, wash them carefully, and freeze to use as needed. Although a little wet when thawed, they are perfectly adequate. If you cannot get any roots, then use an extra length of the lower stalks. Cilantro leaves are now so easy to find that preservation is hardly necessary—the washed plant will keep for a few days in a refrigerator, either wrapped in a plastic bag or in a salad compartment.

Sweet basil *Bai horabha* and Holy basil *Bai krapow*

Both of these are, in fact, varieties of sweet basil. The herb we call "sweet" basil is nearest to the one used in Italian cuisine. Holy basil, with narrower leaves and sometimes a reddish-purple tinge, has a stronger, more intense taste and must be cooked to release its flavor.

There is a third Thai basil, *bai manglak* or lemon-scented basil, which has slightly hairy, paler green leaves. It is delicious, but very fragile and it cannot be exported easily, so you are unlikely to find it outside Thailand.

The more robust sweet and holy basils can be dried and do not have to be soaked before using. While some of the flavor will be lost in the drying process, it is the only way to preserve basil, because the delicate leaves will be damaged if frozen.

Lemongrass *Takrai*

In its natural state, lemongrass is exactly that—a grass, easily recognized by its long, lemon-scented blades. In warm climates, it grows quickly and abundantly, one stalk multiplying to almost 50 in a single season. It will occasionally produce a flower, but even in Thailand this is rare.

Lemongrass is found throughout Southeast Asia, India, Central and South America, and the Caribbean. It can be cultivated under hothouse conditions in temperate climates, but needs great care.

When you find it in a market, the grassy leaves will have been chopped off. What remains is the lower stalk from which the coarsest outer leaves will have been stripped. The pale green, almost white, bulbous stalk, then looks something like a fat scallion or small leek.

Lime, Kaffir lime, and Kaffir lime leaf *Manao, Magrut,* and *Bai magrut*

From a cook's point of view, the essential difference between the light green lime, familiar in the West, and the darker, knobbly kaffir, or wild lime, is juice—the kaffir lime doesn't have any. While all of a lime, zest, and juice, can be used, only the zest of the kaffir lime is serviceable. The reason kaffir lime is so much liked in Thailand is that its zest has a far more intense flavor than its lighter cousin. Indeed, we think there is little difference between a lemon and an ordinary lime (we use the same word, *manao*, for both). You can peel a kaffir lime and freeze the zest for future use.

We also use the leaves of the kaffir lime as a herb. They are much appreciated for the pungent lemony aroma they give to a dish. They too can be frozen or dried, and are used in the way that bay leaves are in the West. Unless otherwise specified, the kaffir lime leaves in the recipes in this book are fresh. Where dry leaves are used, they need not be soaked but can be put straight into the mixture in the same way as bay leaves.

Small red or green chiles
Prik khee noo suan

The Thai name for these tiny red or green chiles (about ½ inch long) means "mouse droppings." They are much appreciated for their intense heat. Because they do not keep well, you are unlikely to find them outside Southeast Asia, because exporters prefer to send the next largest size.

Bird's eye chiles
Pri khee noo

Slightly larger bird's eye chiles, about 1 inch long, are marginally less hot, but still pretty fiendish.

Large red or green chiles
Prik chee faa

These fresh red or green chiles are 3–4 inches long. They are slightly less hot than the small varieties.

Garlic Kratiam

Garlic is an essential part of most Thai dishes. It is used whole, chopped, crushed, raw, stir-fried, fried, and pickled. Thai garlic cloves are small with a thin papery skin, which is why we often do no more than crush them with a heavy blow from the side of a cleaver before tossing them, skins included, into the pan. With non-Thai garlic you will have to peel off the skin.

The first use of garlic in Thai cooking is to flavor the cooking oil before sautéing meat or vegetables. We never use oils that carry their own flavor, such as olive oil, and only rarely use sesame oil. Mostly we prefer bland vegetable oils, such as peanut oil.

Some dishes call for garlic to be fried in a little oil until golden brown, then reserved to be sprinkled over the finished dish, almost like a final pungent condiment.

Generally, garlic is a hidden flavor, but sometimes it moves to center stage, cut into ovals and deep-fried to add a rich taste and crisp texture. Where a really strong flavor is required, we use pickled garlic.

Buy garlic that is firm to the touch and seems heavy for its size—a slight pinkish tinge is a good sign. Garlic keeps well in a cool, dry, well-ventilated place, but should not be stored in the refrigerator where it may become mildewed or start to sprout.

Shallots Hom daeng

The shallot is a sweeter and milder member of the onion family. Thai shallots are so sweet we sometimes use them in sweet dishes. Shallots are best when small, with coppery-pink skins, which should be peeled like regular onions. Some varieties come in tight clusters like large garlic cloves, and must be pulled apart. Avoid the very large varieties that sometimes appear, because these can be as strongly flavored as the average onion, which rather misses the point. Small shallots are sold loose or tied in bundles. They should be firm and without any sprouts or blemishes or signs of rot. Like garlic, they keep well in a cool, dry, well-ventilated place, but may sprout in the refrigerator.

Ginger King

Ginger, often called "root ginger" or "ginger root," was until recently more often seen as preserved sweet ginger in jars or as ground ginger, which could be rather musty and unpleasant. Fortunately, the knobbly, golden-beige "fingers" of fresh ginger are now quite common in markets and supermarkets.

An infusion of ginger and water is good for stomach disorders, including morning sickness during pregnancy. It is also taken as a stimulant.

There are several varieties of ginger grown in Thailand, each with its own unique properties. Young fresh ginger is also available and is still tender enough to be stir-fried like a vegetable. In Thai cuisine, ginger is often eaten raw as a spicy nibble with dips or sausages. For this purpose, use only the youngest, most tender rhizomes—older ginger is too fibrous and dry, although it is quite acceptable if cooked. Recipes usually recommend that you peel a piece of fresh ginger, then sliver it into thin matchsticks so it will cook thoroughly and be easily digestible.

If you find any young ginger (it will be pinker in color) you should rush to buy it. Whether young or old, choose roots that are firm and not shriveled or marked. Wrapped well in plastic wrap, ginger can be kept in the refrigerator for up to 2 weeks.

Galangal Khaa

This rhizome was immensely popular in late medieval Europe, but has not been much used in Western cooking since. It is now returning, thanks to the popularity of Asian cuisines. Like its cousin ginger, it is good for stomach problems, especially nausea. While slightly harder than ginger, it is used in exactly the same way— peeled and slivered into matchsticks or finely sliced into thin rounds in order to cook thoroughly.

Galangal is widely available in markets selling Southeast Asian produce. Fresh ginger is used as a common substitute in the West, though it has a totally different flavor and the recipes will not taste the same.

Well wrapped, galangal will keep in the refrigerator for 2 weeks, or it can be frozen and used from frozen.

Coconut cream and milk Ma prow

Coconut cream and the thinner coconut milk are available in a number of forms. Authentically, of course, they are made from fresh mature coconuts, but there are a number of short cuts. You can buy blocks of coconut, which are not unlike blocks of white wax; these are heated according to the instructions on the package and dissolve into a cream. You can also buy powdered coconut milk, which again includes instructions on adding water to produce the desired liquid mixture. I cannot recommend either of these products, because the manufacturers tend to adulterate the coconut with flour, and this produces a somewhat stale flavor. By far the best short cut is to use cans of coconut cream or milk, which are easily available and made from fresh mature coconuts. Some brands do add a little flour, but not enough to spoil the flavor. If a recipe specifies coconut cream, and you have only coconut milk, don't shake the can. When opened, you will find it separated into thick cream at one end, and thinner milk at the other. Carefully spoon off the cream for use in the recipe.

Fish sauce Nam pla

This is the main flavoring in Thai cooking, for which there is no substitute. It is the same salty seasoning used in Ancient Rome where a similar liquid called "garum" or "liquamen" was used before it was replaced by salt. Although it can also be made with shrimp, fish sauce is most commonly the thin brown liquid extracted from salted, fermented fish. The best is homemade and is a light whiskey color with a refreshing salty taste rather than being dark, with a heavy, bitter tang and a powerful fishy aroma.

When buying commercially produced fish sauce, I try to find a lighter rather than a darker liquid. Color is also the best way to judge whether a bottle has been open for too long, because the sauce darkens with age. It should be discarded if it has changed color significantly. Other than that, there is little to choose between the different producers and their country of origin—Thailand, Vietnam, and China all produce good fish sauce. While some people prefer not to buy it in plastic containers, I doubt whether that makes any difference—go by the color if anything.

Light and dark soy sauce *Siew*
These are Chinese sauces made from salted, cooked soy beans fermented with flour, after which the liquid is extracted. There are several varieties and, while all are "meaty" in flavor, they vary in color and intensity from light to dark brown or almost black. Commercially, only two varieties are available: light soy sauce, which is thin with a clear, delicate flavor, mild enough to be used as a condiment at table, and dark soy sauce which is thicker with a stronger, sweeter flavor, having been fermented with other ingredients such as mushrooms and ginger that darken the final liquid. However, the difference between light and dark is slight, with dark being used more to color the food than anything. If you rarely cook Asian food, you will probably need only a bottle of the more common light soy sauce.

Oyster sauce *Nam man hoy*
This thick brown liquid is also of Chinese origin and is made from oysters that have been cooked in soy sauce and then mixed with seasonings and brine. The result does not, however, taste of fish, as might be expected. It is sold in bottles and somewhat resembles brown ketchup. If used rarely, it should be stored in the refrigerator.

Bean sauce *Tow jiew*
Bean sauces consist of slightly mashed fermented soy beans—black or yellow. They help thicken a dish as well as add flavor. Black bean sauce is thick and deeply colored and is used to give a richer flavor than even dark soy sauce can achieve.

Yellow bean sauce is more salty and pungent, but again, this is a quite subtle refinement. If you cook Thai food only occasionally, you may need no more than a jar of black bean sauce. You can, however, get very small cans of both sauces, sufficient for one Thai cooking session. If you can get it only in larger jars, preservation offers no problems as both bean sauces will keep almost indefinitely in the refrigerator.

Chile sauce *Sod prik*
A thick dipping sauce made from a combination of sweet and hot chiles, pulped and mixed with vinegar, garlic, and other spices.

Chile powder *Prik pon*
A red powder made by grinding small dried red chiles (*prik khee noo haeng*). In Thailand it is sold in jars, packages, or cardboard containers.

Shrimp paste *Kapee*
Because it is full of protein and is a good source of vitamin B, shrimp paste is a staple for many of Asia's poor, whose diet consists of boiled rice flavored with this pungent preserve. The paste is made by pounding shrimp with salt and leaving them to decompose. It is sold both dried and "fresh," a slight misnomer when what is really meant is "not dried."

The "fresh" *kapee* is shrimp pink and can be bought in jars in the West, though it is difficult to find. It should be stored in the refrigerator. The sun-dried variety is dark purple from the black eyes of the kheu shrimp, but be wary if it is too dark as this may mean that dye has been added. Dried *kapee* is stronger than fresh, but once again it should not be painfully salty. It can be kept without refrigerating. Rayong produces the best dried *kapee*.

Both fresh and dried shrimp paste have a disturbingly powerful aroma and you should remove what you want from the jar as quickly as possible in case the bad smells escape into your kitchen. Fortunately this odor disappears when the *kapee* is cooked.

You can use either fresh or dried shrimp paste in a recipe. Unless otherwise stated, my recipes all call for dried *kapee*. If substituting fresh, use double the quantity listed. If none can be found, you could use Western anchovy paste—about half the amount of the dried shrimp paste required.

Dried shrimp *Gung Haeng*
These are not preserved shrimp waiting to be reconstituted in water and used as a seafood ingredient in a dish. Instead they should be considered more as a dry flavoring that is especially good with blander ingredients such as cabbage and tofu. Ideally, dried shrimp should be tiny, a natural shrimp pink and not too salty. This flavoring is made by boiling and peeling shrimp, then spreading them out in the sun to dry. The end result is sold loose, in jars, or plastic bags. Dried shrimp can be kept for a long time, though they may turn slightly moist, in which case they must be either sun-dried again or dry-heated briefly in the oven.

Look out for a special version from the southern city of Songkla. These shrimp are not peeled but are dried in their shells. They are good deep-fried, after which the shells become crisp and edible, ready to be served as a appetizer.

Palm sugar *Nam tan peep*
Palm sugar is produced from the sap of various kinds of palm. The commonest are the coconut palm and the sugar palm, each of which gives a slightly different flavor, though the standard commercial product, sold in cans or cakes, has a fairly uniform taste. The unique quality of palm sugar is its deep caramel flavor, quite different from ordinary cane sugar.

If coconut sap is left to ferment for just a day you get palm wine or palm toddy, a highly alcoholic beverage. If the sap is boiled down until it crystallizes, you get a coarse sticky sugar. The deep flavor of palm sugar adds a distinctive edge to Thai confections, but it is also used to add another dimension to savory dishes such as curries.

If you plan to use only a little at a time, you should try to buy well-compressed cakes of palm sugar, because these will keep for a long time in a well-sealed jar. The best is soft brown in color and has a distinctive toffee-like aroma. You should be able to find it without difficulty in Asian stores or by mail order (page 142).

RICE *Khao*
Fragrant Thai rice (jasmine rice)

These are the names under which Thai rice is sold abroad. It is a long-grain, jasmine-scented rice and is of the highest quality. It is served boiled or steamed and can be reheated in a variety of ways, most often fried.

BOILED RICE *KHAO SUAY*

1 lb. (2¾ cups) Thai fragrant rice
2¾ cups water

makes 7 cups

An experienced Thai cook varies the water according to the age and dryness of the rice, but the above is a reasonable average ratio.

Rinse the rice thoroughly at least 3 times in cold water until the water runs clear. Put the rice in a heavy saucepan and add the water. Cover and quickly bring to a boil. Uncover and cook, stirring vigorously, until the water level is below that of the rice (the surface will begin to look dry). Turn the heat as low as possible, cover the pan again (put a layer of foil under the lid, if necessary, to ensure a tight fit), and steam for 20 minutes.

The good news is that none of this is really necessary. Buy a rice cooker: they are cheap, super-efficient, and make and keep perfect rice with absolutely no fuss or bother.

Sticky or glutinous rice *Khao niew*

This is a broad, short-grain rice, mostly white, although sometimes brown or even black. As its name implies, it is the opposite of light and fluffy, being thick and almost porridgy. It is the staple of northern Thailand where during a meal it is plucked with the fingers, rolled into a ball, and used to scoop up the other food.

Sticky rice is also used throughout Thailand to make sweet dishes, and it is milled into rice flour which is bought ready-ground.

Sticky rice cannot be cooked in an electric rice-steamer and must be soaked before cooking.

STEAMED STICKY RICE *KHAO NIEW*

1 lb. (2¾ cups) glutinous or sticky rice

makes 7 cups

Soak the rice in water to cover for at least 3 hours or overnight. Drain and rinse thoroughly.

Line the perforated part of a steamer with a double thickness of cheesecloth and add the soaked rice. Heat water in the bottom of the steamer to boiling, then steam the rice over moderate heat for 30 minutes.

utensils

It is quite easy to cook Thai food using utensils available in most Western kitchens: a skillet instead of a wok, a blender instead of a mortar and pestle, steaming rice in a pan rather than using a rice cooker, and so on. If, after trying a few recipes, you decide that you are going to cook Thai food on a more regular basis, it would be wise to invest in some more specialized equipment. This will just make cooking Thai food easier, and more fun.

The basic equipment for setting up a Thai kitchen would be:
- a wok
- a wooden spatula
- a rice cooker
- a wooden chopping block
- a cleaver
- a stone mortar and pestle for crushing herbs and chiles and making pastes.

There are many other "speciality" items, but these will give you a good basis. However, it is not necessary to have these items in order to cook Thai food.

APPETIZERS AND
PARTY BITES

Thai dips are mostly made from chiles. You find them in all regions of Thailand—served with raw or boiled vegetables, sticky rice in the north, and steamed rice in the Central Regions. This dip, as its name implies, is made from young, green, strongly flavored chiles and is wonderful to serve with drinks at parties. In Thailand, dips are used both as dipping sauces, and as sauces for spooning over rice or other dishes, and this is how I have used them in this book.

vegetables with spicy dip of young chiles
nam prik num

4 large fresh green chiles

4 small fresh green chiles

6 large garlic cloves

6 pink Thai shallots or 3 regular ones

4 medium tomatoes

2 tablespoons freshly squeezed lime or lemon juice

2 tablespoons light soy sauce

½ teaspoon salt

2 teaspoons sugar

to serve

your choice of crisp lettuce, cucumber, radishes, celery, or other raw or blanched vegetables

aluminum foil

serves 4

Wrap the chiles, garlic, shallots, and tomatoes in foil and put under a preheated medium broiler. Cook until they begin to soften, turning once or twice. Unwrap, then pound with a mortar and pestle to form a liquid paste.

Add the lemon juice, soy sauce, salt, and sugar to the paste, stirring well, then spoon into a small dipping bowl.

Serve as a dipping sauce, surrounded by crisp salad ingredients, such as lettuce, cucumber, radish, and celery, or with raw or blanched vegetables.

Note In Thailand, we never discard the seeds from chiles, but you can do so if you wish. All chiles vary in heat, so we always work to taste, using more or less, according to our preference.

This recipe originates in the Central Regions of Thailand. It has a richer mix of ingredients, and so would have been a dish found in richer families, possibly of Chinese extraction, as we can see the Chinese influence in the use of yellow bean sauce. It has a mild sweetness and is less spicy than northern dishes. The recipe makes a crisp, fresh appetizer for a Thai meal, but is also easy to eat if you serve it with drinks before dinner or for parties.

crudités with spicy yellow bean sauce dip

tow jiew lon

crisp vegetables of your choice, such as endive, lettuce hearts, green beans, and asparagus

spicy yellow bean sauce dip

2 tablespoons yellow bean sauce, drained to remove excess liquid

1 cup coconut milk

4 pink Thai shallots or 2 regular ones, finely chopped

4 oz. ground pork

4 oz. ground shrimp

2 tablespoons lemon or lime juice

2 teaspoons sugar

1 tablespoon Thai fish sauce

2 large fresh red chiles, sliced lengthwise into fine matchsticks

serves 4

To make the crudités, separate or slice the vegetables into small, convenient portions, arrange on a serving platter, and set aside. If using vegetables such as beans and asparagus, blanch them in a saucepan of boiling salted water first, then cool under cold running water.

To make the dip, use a mortar and pestle to pound the drained yellow beans briefly to break them up a little. Set aside.

Put the coconut milk in a saucepan and heat, stirring until smooth—do not let boil. Add the mashed yellow beans and stir well. Add the shallots, pork, shrimp, lemon juice, sugar, and fish sauce. Bring to a boil and simmer briefly. Remove from the heat, transfer to a food processor, and pulse to blend coarsely. Stir in the chile matchsticks, pour into a bowl, and serve with the crudités.

While I am not a vegetarian myself, this vegetarian dish is a favorite at parties. Thai people consider sesame seeds good for the hair—regular consumption is said keep it strong and shiny, and possibly even maintain the natural blackness longer. Perhaps other hair colors would also benefit.

1¼ cups (2½ oz.) small white mushrooms, halved

1 small sweet potato, halved and sliced

2–3 small carrots, halved lengthwise

2–3 small zucchini, sliced diagonally

a handful of basil leaves

peanut or safflower oil, for deep-frying

batter

¾ cup all-purpose flour

½ teaspoon salt

2 large eggs

1 tablespoon sesame seeds

dipping sauce

¼ cup light soy sauce

½ teaspoon sugar

1 teaspoon coarsely chopped cilantro

1 teaspoon finely chopped fresh ginger

an electric deep-fryer (optional)

serves 4

vegetable fritters with sesame seeds
pak chup bang tod

To make the batter, put the flour and salt in a bowl and mix well. Break the egg into the bowl, add the sesame seeds, and mix thoroughly. Gradually add about 1¼ cups water, whisking constantly. You should have a batter with the thickness of cream.

Heat the peanut oil in a wok or deep-fryer until a light haze appears. Dip each vegetable into the batter, making sure it is thoroughly coated, then slip it into the hot oil. Deep-fry until golden brown. Remove from the oil with a slotted spoon, drain on paper towels, then arrange on a serving dish.

To make the dipping sauce, put the soy sauce, sugar, cilantro, and ginger in a bowl and stir well. Serve with the vegetables.

People have largely forgotten that this so-called traditional Thai dish originated in India. As a child, I remember it being sold by the Indian community. However, it has been adapted to Thai taste by the addition of more fresh chiles. It is a beautiful and elegant dish of many fascinating flavors. Even better—it is easy to make and your vegetarian guests will be delighted that you have catered for them so deliciously.

deep-fried yellow bean balls with thick sweet sauce

baa yir

1 cup (8 oz.) dried split mung beans, soaked in water for 30 minutes and drained

1 tablespoon all-purpose flour

1 teaspoon Red Curry Paste (page 141)

2 tablespoons light soy sauce

2 teaspoons sugar

5 kaffir lime leaves, rolled into a cylinder and finely sliced into slivers

peanut or safflower oil, for deep-frying

thick sweet sauce

¼ cup sugar

⅓ cup rice vinegar

½ teaspoon salt

an electric deep-fryer (optional)

serves 4

To make the sauce, put the sugar, vinegar, and salt in a small saucepan or wok and heat gently until the sugar dissolves. Let cool before serving with the bean balls.

To make the balls, pound the drained mung beans with a mortar and pestle or use a blender to form a coarse paste. Stirring well after each addition, add the flour, curry paste, soy sauce, sugar, and lime leaves. Pluck a small piece of the paste and form into a ball the size of a walnut. Do not mold too tightly.

Fill a wok or deep-fryer one-third full with the oil or to the manufacturer's recommended level. Heat until a scrap of noodle will puff up immediately.

Working in batches if necessary, add the balls and fry until golden brown. Remove with a slotted spoon, drain, and serve with the thick sweet sauce.

Everywhere in Thailand, fish cakes are a favorite traditional dish. While they are simple to make, they are an excellent benchmark of the good Thai cook. With a bit of practice, you will be able to create a cake of just the right texture and consistency. In the old days, the fish and curry paste would have been pounded by hand for a long time with a mortar and pestle, until the cook was happy that the mix was perfect. These days, we can use modern equipment like blenders and food processors and still produce a delicious and aromatic dish.

fish cakes
tod man pla

1 lb. white fish fillets, such as cod, haddock, or halibut

2 tablespoons Red Curry Paste (page 141)

2 tablespoons Thai fish sauce

¾ cup (2½ oz.) very finely sliced thin green beans or Chinese long beans

5 kaffir lime leaves, finely chopped

peanut or safflower oil, for frying

cucumber relish

1 cup rice vinegar

2 tablespoons sugar

2-inch piece of cucumber (unpeeled), coarsely chopped

1 small carrot, chopped

3 pink Thai shallots or 1 regular, finely sliced

1 medium fresh red chile, finely sliced

1 tablespoon crushed roasted peanuts (optional)

an electric deep-fryer (optional)

makes 20 cakes

To make the relish, put the vinegar and sugar in a saucepan and heat, stirring until the sugar dissolves. Boil to produce a thin syrup. Remove from the heat and let cool.

When cool, add the cucumber, carrot, shallots, chile, and peanuts, if using, to the syrup. Mix thoroughly and set aside.

To grind the fish, cut the fillets into pieces and put in a food processor or blender. Pulse to form a smooth paste, then transfer to a large bowl.

Put the curry paste in the bowl and, using your fingers, blend thoroughly with the ground fish. Add the fish sauce, green beans, and kaffir lime leaves and knead together. Shape into small flat cakes about 2 inches across and ½ inch thick.

Fill a wok or deep-fryer one-third full with the oil or to the manufacturer's recommended level. Heat until a scrap of noodle will puff up immediately.

Working in batches if necessary, add the fish cakes and fry until golden brown on both sides. Remove with a slotted spoon and drain on paper towels. Serve the fish cakes with the cucumber relish.

This is one of the most popular appetizers in my restaurant. I think it is the best combination of shrimp and corn and is the first choice when it comes to recommending an appetizer. You can buy plum sauce, but this one is easy to make and goes with many other dishes.

shrimp and corn cakes with plum sauce
tod man kung khao pod

20 black peppercorns

3 garlic cloves

½ teaspoon salt

8 oz. peeled raw shrimp, deveined and finely chopped

fresh corn kernels from 3 uncooked ears of corn

1 tablespoon Thai fish sauce

1 teaspoon sugar

peanut or safflower oil, for deep-frying

plum sauce

2 pickled plums

½ cup rice vinegar

⅓ cup sugar

2 small fresh red and green chiles, finely chopped

an electric deep-fryer (optional)

serves 4

To make the sauce, use a fork to scrape the plum flesh from the pit. Put the vinegar in a saucepan, heat gently, then add the sugar and the plum flesh, stirring until the sugar dissolves. Simmer until a thin syrup begins to form, then remove from the heat. Stir in the chiles, then pour into a bowl and set aside.

Using a large mortar and pestle, pound the peppercorns, garlic, and salt to form a paste. Add the shrimp and pound well into the paste. Add the corn, fish sauce, and sugar and pound well. Alternatively, use a food processor.

You should now have a thick paste. Mold the paste into 12 cakes about 1½–2 inches diameter.

Fill a wok or deep-fryer one-third full with the oil or to the manufacturer's recommended level. Heat until a scrap of noodle will puff up immediately.

Working in batches if necessary, fry the cakes until golden brown, then remove with a slotted spoon, drain on paper towels, and serve with the plum sauce.

Note Though you can buy ready-made plum sauce, you can make your own with pickled plums available in jars from Asian foodstores and by mail order (page 142).

Shrimp wrapped in crispy noodles produce a delicious combination—the contrast between the softness of the shrimp and the crisp texture of deep-fried noodles is exceptional. Though this dish looks spectacular, it is not difficult to make. In fact, it's a recipe for the home cook, because it has to be wrapped and fried at the last minute, and doesn't lend itself to the large quantities and advance preparation methods of restaurant chefs.

shrimp wrapped in crispy noodles
gung sarong

1 egg
½ teaspoon salt
½ teaspoon sugar
1½ teaspoons freshly ground white pepper
8 jumbo shrimp, peeled and deveined, tails on
1 nest fresh ba mee noodles
peanut or safflower oil, for deep-frying

sweet and hot sauce
¼ cup rice vinegar
⅓ cup sugar
½ teaspoon salt
2 small red chiles, finely chopped

an electric deep-fryer (optional)

makes 8: serves 4

To make the sauce, put the sugar, vinegar, and salt in a saucepan and heat, stirring until the sugar dissolves. Add the chiles and ¼ cup water, stir well, and simmer until it becomes a thin syrup. Pour into a dipping bowl.

Put the egg, salt, sugar, and pepper in a bowl and beat well. Add the shrimp and mix well. Lift 3–4 strands of noodle and wrap each shrimp, winding the strands into a mesh thickly covering the shrimp.

Fill a wok or deep-fryer one-third full with the oil or to the manufacturer's recommended level. Heat until a scrap of noodle will puff up immediately.

Working in batches if necessary, fry the wrapped shrimp until golden brown. Drain and serve with the sweet and hot sauce or plum sauce (page 24).

Note Ba mee noodles are made from egg and wheat flour and are always sold fresh in "nests." Buy them in Chinese or Southeast Asian markets.

This fascinating dish consists of crab, shrimp, and pork blended into a fusion of different textures. It is a perfect party dish because it sounds and looks interesting—but most importantly, it tastes delicious. Ready-cracked crab claws are sold in Asian stores and at most fishsellers—they are too fiddly to crack yourself.

deep-fried crab claws with pork and shrimp
poo tod

4 oz. ground pork

4 oz. raw shrimp, shelled, deveined and finely chopped

1 large egg, beaten

2 garlic cloves, finely chopped

1 tablespoon Thai fish sauce

1 tablespoon oyster sauce

1 teaspoon cornstarch

½ teaspoon freshly ground white pepper

8 prepared cocktail crab claws (see recipe introduction)

peanut or safflower oil, for deep-frying

Plum Sauce, to serve (page 24)

an electric deep-fryer (optional)

makes 8: serves 4

Put the pork, shrimp, egg, garlic, fish sauce, oyster sauce, cornstarch, and pepper in a bowl.

Divide the mixture by the number of crab claws (8) and mold one portion around the meaty section of each claw, leaving the pincer exposed.

Fill a wok or deep-fryer one-third full with the oil or to the manufacturer's recommended level. Heat until a scrap of noodle will puff up immediately.

Working in batches if necessary, add the coated crab claws, and deep-fry until the molded sections are a deep golden brown. Remove with a slotted spoon, drain, and serve with the plum sauce.

For this dish, only the thick part of the wings (little drumsticks) are used, marinated in a blend of lemongrass and chile. The crunchiness of the deep-fried lemongrass on the little drumsticks makes for an interesting texture. The winglets are simple to prepare. Run a knife around the narrow end of the wing, just below the knuckle, then use your knife to cut and push the flesh down the bone to form a little ball at the bottom. The bone then acts as a handle, making perfect finger food. This recipe is one of my own creation.

chicken wings with lemongrass and sweet and hot sauce

gai ta-krai

3 stalks of lemongrass, finely chopped

2 small chiles, finely chopped

3 tablespoons oyster sauce

1 tablespoon Thai fish sauce

1 teaspoon sugar

1 lb. chicken winglets (also known as drumettes)

peanut or safflower oil, for deep-frying

to serve

Sweet and Hot Sauce (page 27)

sprigs of cilantro

an electric deep-fryer (optional)

serves 4

Put the lemongrass, chiles, oyster sauce, fish sauce, and sugar in a bowl and beat with a fork. Add the chicken winglets, turn to coat, and set aside to marinate for 15 minutes.

Fill a wok or deep-fryer one-third full with the oil or to the manufacturer's recommended level. Heat until a scrap of noodle will puff up immediately.

Working in batches if necessary, fry the chicken wings until golden brown. Remove with a slotted spoon, drain, and serve with sweet and hot sauce and sprigs of cilantro.

Note If you are unable to find chicken winglets, buy the whole wings and cut off the last 2 joints. Use them for another recipe or to make stock.

Thai food has become increasingly popular in the West, and is even served in English pubs! Chicken satay is one of the most popular Thai dishes on any menu. You can use it as part of a barbecue menu, whether Asian or not, or as a party snack—the sticks make this very easy to nibble with drinks, and the peanut sauce is good as a dip with other foods, such as crudités.

chicken satay

satay

2 teaspoons coriander seeds

2 teaspoons cumin seeds

4 skinless chicken breasts

2 tablespoons Thai fish sauce

1 teaspoon salt

¼ cup peanut or safflower oil

1 tablespoon curry powder

1 tablespoon ground turmeric

½ cup coconut milk

3 tablespoons sugar

lemon or lime wedges, to serve

peanut sauce

2 tablespoons peanut or safflower oil

3 garlic cloves, finely chopped

1 tablespoon Panaeng Curry Paste (page 141)

½ cup coconut milk

1 cup chicken stock

1 tablespoon sugar

1 teaspoon salt

2 tablespoons lemon or lime juice

¼ cup crushed roasted peanuts

8-inch wooden skewers, soaked in cold water for about 30 minutes

serves 4

To make the peanut sauce, heat the oil in a skillet until a light haze appears. Add the chopped garlic and sauté until golden brown. Add the curry paste, mix well, and cook for a few seconds. Add the coconut milk, mix well, and cook for a few seconds more. Add the stock, sugar, salt, and lemon juice and stir to blend. Cook for 1–2 minutes, constantly stirring. Add the ground peanuts, stir thoroughly, and pour the sauce into a bowl.

To make the satays, toast the coriander and cumin seeds gently in a small skillet without oil for about 5 minutes, stirring and shaking to make sure they don't burn. Remove from the heat and grind with a mortar and pestle to make a fine powder. (You could substitute ready-ground seeds if that is more convenient.)

Using a sharp knife, cut the chicken breasts lengthwise into thin strips, about ⅛ inch wide. Put them in a bowl and add the ground toasted seeds, fish sauce, salt, peanut oil, curry powder, turmeric, coconut milk, and sugar. Mix thoroughly, cover with plastic wrap, and refrigerate for 8 hours or overnight (you can prepare them in the morning to serve in the evening).

Preheat a broiler or outdoor grill. Thread 2 pieces of the marinated chicken onto each skewer—not straight through the meat, but rather as if you were gathering or smocking a piece of fabric in a zigzag fashion. Grill or broil the satays until the meat is cooked through—6–8 minutes—turning to make sure they are browned on both sides. Serve with the peanut sauce and perhaps a few lemon or lime wedges.

I well remember this dish as one of my father's favorites—my mother often prepared it as an afternoon snack. It makes excellent finger food for parties and often appears on Thai restaurant menus as an appetizer. It can be served on its own or alternatively with a hot sauce to add a more spicy flavor.

pork toasts
kanom bang na moo

6 slices of white bread, crusts trimmed and each slice cut into 4

4 small garlic cloves, finely chopped

3 cilantro roots, chopped

8 oz. ground pork

1 extra-large egg

2 tablespoons Thai fish sauce

a pinch of freshly ground white pepper

peanut or safflower oil, for deep-frying

to serve

cilantro leaves

about 2 inches cucumber, quartered lengthwise, then thinly sliced crosswise

1 fresh red chile, finely sliced into rings

a baking sheet

an electric deep-fryer (optional)

serves 4

Preheat the oven to 250°F. Arrange the pieces of bread on a baking sheet, put in the oven for 5 minutes, then remove.

Meanwhile, using a mortar and pestle or blender, either pound or grind the garlic and cilantro roots together. Put in a bowl, then add the pork, egg, fish sauce, and white pepper and mix thoroughly. Put 1 teaspoon of the mixture on each piece of toast.

Fill a wok or deep-fryer one-third full with the oil or to the manufacturer's recommended level. Heat until a scrap of noodle will puff up immediately.

Working in batches of 2–3 at a time, fry the toasts for 2–3 minutes until browned. Remove with a slotted spoon, drain on paper towels, then arrange on a large plate and serve with the cilantro, cucumber, and chile.

This is a traditional dish from the northeast of Thailand and goes especially well with Steamed Sticky Rice (page 11) and Papaya Salad with Squid (page 54). The marinade of coriander seeds and cilantro roots helps to create a uniquely sweet flavor. For best results, the pork is cooked over charcoal, so makes an ideal dish for barbecues. Otherwise cook under a broiler or on a stove-top grill pan.

skewered marinated pork

moo ping

1 teaspoon coriander seeds

4 garlic cloves, finely chopped

6 cilantro roots, finely chopped

¼ cup Thai fish sauce

2 tablespoons light soy sauce

1 cup thick coconut cream

2 tablespoons peanut or safflower oil

1 tablespoon sugar

½ teaspoon freshly ground white pepper

1 lb. lean pork, thinly sliced
into pieces about 3 x 2 inches

lettuce, parsley, or cilantro, to serve

sauce

2 tablespoons Thai fish sauce

2 tablespoons lemon or lime juice

1 tablespoon light soy sauce

1 teaspoon chile powder

1 tablespoon sugar

1 tablespoon coarsely chopped
fresh cilantro

*12 long wooden skewers, 6–8 inches,
soaked in cold water for at least 30 minutes*

makes 12 skewers: serves 4–12

Using a mortar and pestle, pound the coriander seeds, garlic, and cilantro roots together in turn to form a paste. Then mix in the fish sauce, soy sauce, coconut cream, oil, sugar, and pepper until thoroughly blended. Add the pork and stir well, making sure that each piece is thoroughly coated. Let stand for at least 30 minutes, but longer if possible.

To make the sauce, while the meat is marinating, put the fish sauce, lemon juice, soy sauce, chile powder, sugar, and cilantro in a small bowl and mix well. Taste—if too hot, add more fish sauce, lemon juice, and sugar.

Preheat a broiler or outdoor grill. Thread 2 pieces of meat onto each skewer, making sure that as much of the surface of the meat as possible will be exposed to the heat. (Make more skewers if you have meat left over.) Broil or grill at a high heat for 2–3 minutes on each side, or until the meat is thoroughly cooked through. Serve on a platter with lettuce, parsley, or cilantro, with the sauce on the side.

SOUPS AND SALADS

This vegetarian soup is one I have developed in my own restaurants to meet the demand for something a little different and delicious for our many vegetarian customers. While cauliflower is familiar as an ingredient in stir fry recipes, prized for its crunchiness, here it is cooked with mushrooms and coconut milk, so the cauliflower absorbs the flavor of coconut, making it light and sweet.

cauliflower, mushroom, and coconut soup

tom kay jay

2¾ cups (28 oz. can) coconut cream

2 stalks of lemongrass, finely sliced

2 inches fresh galangal or ginger, peeled and finely sliced into rings

4 kaffir lime leaves, coarsely torn into quarters

1 small cauliflower, cut into florets

2½ cups small white mushrooms, cut into halves or quarters, according to size

3 tablespoons light soy sauce

1 teaspoon sugar

2¾ cups vegetable stock

4 fresh small red or green chiles, slightly crushed

3 tablespoons lemon or lime juice

cilantro leaves, to serve

serves 4

Put the coconut cream, lemongrass, galangal, kaffir lime leaves, cauliflower, mushrooms, soy sauce, sugar, and stock in a large saucepan and bring to a boil. Reduce the heat and simmer until the cauliflower florets are *al dente* (cooked, but still firm). Remove from the heat and add the chiles and lemon juice. Stir once, pour into a serving bowl, and top with cilantro.

Notes If you are unable to find cans or cartons of coconut cream, use canned coconut milk instead. Don't shake the can—you will find it has probably separated into thick cream and thin milk. Carefully spoon off the thick part to use in recipes that specify coconut cream.

Galangal is widely available in Asian food stores and sometimes in larger supermarkets. Fresh ginger is used as a common substitute in the West, though it has a totally different flavor and the recipes will not taste the same. You can order galangal from one of the sources on page 142 and freeze until ready to use.

Thai food has become popular because it offers such a variety of tastes, flavors, and textures—more than in other cuisines. This single soup combines many of those flavors and textures, giving you a typical taste of Thailand.

sweet and sour tofu soup
gaeng preowan bu

5 cups vegetable stock

1 tablespoon cornstarch

2½ oz. pickled cabbage, chopped into 1-inch lengths

2½ oz. bamboo shoots, cut into matchsticks

4–5 ears of baby corn, chopped into rings

½ cup (2 oz.) shelled peas, fresh or frozen

4 oz. silken tofu, cut into ¼-inch cubes

½ cup (about 3 oz.) lump crabmeat

½ small red or green bell pepper, finely chopped

2 tablespoons light soy sauce

2 tablespoons Thai fish sauce

1 tablespoon vinegar, preferably red vinegar

1 teaspoon sugar

½ teaspoon freshly ground white pepper

cilantro leaves, to serve

serves 4

Put the stock in a large saucepan and bring to a boil. Mix the cornstarch in a small bowl with about 1 tablespoon water, then stir the mixture into the stock to thicken it slightly.

Add the cabbage, bamboo shoots and corn, then stir in the peas, tofu, crabmeat, bell pepper, soy sauce, fish sauce, red vinegar, sugar, and white pepper, stirring constantly.

Ladle at once into a serving bowl and top with cilantro leaves.

Note Red vinegar is available in Asian stores. If you can't find it, use white.

Although Westerners like to have soup as a separate course, in Thailand it is served with other dishes. People ladle spoonfuls of soup from a communal bowl onto the rice on their plates. There are two main categories of soup—spicy like this one and plain like the one on page 49. Tom Yam Kung is a traditional Thai soup, with an aroma created by kaffir lime leaves and lemongrass. It is definitely a must on the menu in all Thai restaurants, and easy to make at home.

hot and sour soup with shrimp
tom yam kung

5 cups chicken stock

1 tablespoon tom yam sauce

4 kaffir lime leaves, finely chopped

2 stalks of tender lemongrass, coarsely sliced

3 tablespoons freshly squeezed lemon or lime juice

3 tablespoons Thai fish sauce

2 small fresh red or green chiles, finely sliced

2 teaspoons sugar

12 straw mushrooms, halved (canned mushrooms will do)

12 raw jumbo shrimp, shelled and deveined, tail fins left on

serves 4

Heat the stock in a saucepan and add the tom yam sauce. Stir in the lime leaves, lemongrass, lemon juice, fish sauce, chiles, and sugar. Bring to a boil and simmer for 2 minutes. Add the mushrooms and shrimp, stir and cook for a further 2–3 minutes, or until the shrimp are cooked through. Ladle into soup bowls and serve.

Note Tom yam sauce is widely available, even in some supermarkets. If you can't find it, try an Asian store, or buy mail order from one of the sources on page 142.

This is a staple dish in the Thai diet, whenever we want something filling to eat at unusual hours. Rice soup is to the Thai breakfast menu what cereals are in the West. Then, at the other end of the day, it continues to provide a quick source of sustenance, when revelers stop for a middle-of-the-night bowl of rice soup at any of the 24-hour food stalls you find in Thai cities.

chicken rice soup
khaotom gai

2 tablespoons peanut or safflower oil

2 garlic cloves, coarsely chopped

5 cups chicken stock

3 cups cooked rice
(from about 1 cup raw rice)

1 lb. boneless skinless chicken breasts
or thighs, thinly sliced

1 teaspoon chopped
preserved vegetables (tang chi)

2 tablespoons Thai fish sauce

2 tablespoons soy sauce

1 teaspoon sugar

1 inch fresh ginger,
peeled and cut into fine shreds

½ teaspoon freshly ground white pepper

to serve

1 scallion, finely sliced

a few fresh cilantro leaves

serves 4

Heat the oil in a small skillet, add the garlic, and sauté until golden brown. Set aside to infuse, reserving both the oil and the garlic.

Heat the stock in a large saucepan, add the cooked rice and slices of chicken, and bring to a boil.

Stir in the preserved vegetables, fish sauce, soy sauce, sugar, ginger, and white pepper and simmer gently for about 30 seconds, or until the chicken is cooked through.

Transfer to a serving bowl and trickle over a little of the reserved garlic oil. Top with finely sliced scallion and fresh cilantro leaves.

Note In Thailand, we always make this from leftover rice—we don't start from scratch. Keep leftover rice in the refrigerator and use it as soon as possible for dishes like this rice soup and for fried rice.

While Tom Yam is well known in Western countries, Tom Som is less so, although it is an equal favorite inside Thailand. However, that lack of familiarity in the West can change because the ingredients are now more widely available. The sparerib-based stock includes a mixture of garlic, shallots, ginger, and tamarind water—the latter contributing its strong, sour taste. It offers an exciting alternative to the traditional Tom Yam soup.

sparerib and tamarind soup

tom som

1 teaspoon black peppercorns

1 tablespoon finely chopped cilantro root

2 garlic cloves

4 pink Thai shallots or 2 regular ones

1 tablespoon peanut or safflower oil

5 cups chicken stock

1 lb. small pork spareribs, chopped into 1-inch pieces

2 inches fresh ginger, finely sliced into matchsticks

2 tablespoons tamarind water

2 tablespoons sugar

3 tablespoons Thai fish sauce

4 scallions, chopped into 1-inch lengths

serves 4

Using a mortar and pestle, pound the peppercorns, cilantro root, garlic, and shallots to form a paste.

Heat the oil in a large saucepan, add the paste, and sauté for 5 seconds, stirring well. Add the stock and bring to a boil, stirring well. Add the spareribs and return to a boil.

Add the ginger, tamarind water, sugar, fish sauce, and scallions. Return to a boil again and simmer for 1 minute. Ladle into a bowl and serve.

Note Preparing tamarind

If you can't find tamarind water, or the pulp to make it, tamarind paste is available in small bottles in Asian stores. For this recipe, mix 1 tablespoon paste with 1 tablespoon water.

Tamarind pulp is also available in block form. To prepare your own tamarind water, mix 1 tablespoon tamarind pulp in a bowl with ⅔ cup hot water, mashing with a fork. As you mix the pulp and water, the water absorbs the taste of the tamarind. When the water is cool, you can squeeze the tamarind pulp to extract more juice (and you can remove any seeds). Pour off the juice into a container and set aside for use in recipes. It will keep for about a week in the refrigerator.

This vegetarian salad looks like any Western salad. However, just like all other salads, the magical ingredient that makes it unique is the dressing. From my point of view, the dressing for this salad is as good as any found in Western cuisines.

peanut or safflower oil, for deep-frying

2 blocks of firm tofu, about 2 inches square

1 cup (4 oz.) bean sprouts, rinsed, drained, and trimmed

1 cup (4 oz.) Chinese long beans, chopped into 1-inch lengths

2 medium tomatoes, thinly sliced

1 cup (4 oz.) thinly sliced cucumber

1 cup (4 oz.) thinly sliced white cabbage, broken into strands

2 hard-cooked large eggs, shelled and quartered

peanut dressing

2 tablespoons peanut or safflower oil

1 tablespoon Red Curry Paste (page 141)

1¼ cups coconut milk

½ teaspoon salt

1 tablespoon sugar

¼ cup crushed peanuts

serves 4

vegetable salad with peanut dressing
salad kaek

To make the dressing, heat the oil in a wok or skillet and stir in the curry paste. Add the coconut milk and stir well. Add the salt, sugar, and peanuts and stir well. Cook briefly until the coconut milk comes to a boil. Remove immediately from the heat.

To make the salad, fill a wok or saucepan about one-third full with the peanut oil and heat until a scrap of noodle will fluff up immediately. Using a slotted spoon, add the tofu to the hot oil and deep-fry until golden. Remove with a slotted spoon, drain on paper towels, and set aside.

Arrange all the vegetables and eggs in a salad bowl. Thinly slice the tofu and put the slices in the bowl. Serve with the dressing, either separately, or poured over the salad and tossed.

In Thailand, yam (salad) is essential in every meal. A yam is a mixture of many different ingredients and flavors. It can include vegetables, meats, shellfish, fish, and herbs and is always spicy.

seafood salad
yam talay

crisp lettuce leaves, such as romaine hearts

1 small onion, thinly sliced and separated into rings

½ cup (4 oz.) pineapple chunks

½ cup (4 oz.) shelled mussels

½ cup (4 oz.) shelled baby clams

4 oz. baby squid, chopped into small rings

4 oz. peeled raw shrimp, deveined and halved lengthwise

4 oz. fish balls, halved

cilantro, to serve

salad dressing

2 garlic cloves, very finely chopped

4 small red or green chiles, very finely chopped

2 tablespoons roasted peanuts, crushed

1 tablespoon sugar

3 tablespoons Thai fish sauce

3 tablespoons freshly squeezed lime juice

serves 4

To make the dressing, put the garlic, chiles, peanuts, sugar, fish sauce, and lime juice in a bowl and mix well. Set aside.

To make the salad, put the lettuce leaves, onion rings, and pineapple chunks in a large serving bowl and set aside.

Pour about 1 cup water in a saucepan, bring to a boil, then add the squid, shrimp, and fish balls. Return to a boil for 1–2 minutes, just until the shrimp are opaque. Do not overcook or the seafood will be tough. Remove immediately with a slotted spoon and put in a mixing bowl.

Rinse out the saucepan, add the squid, shrimp, mussels, clams, and fish balls, and pour over the prepared dressing. Heat and stir briefly, just long enough to reheat the seafood, no more than a minute. Spoon the seafood and dressing into the bowl of lettuce, toss well, top with cilantro, and serve.

Notes If using unshelled mussels and clams, you will need about 8 oz. of each. Heat a little water in a large saucepan, add the cleaned mussels, put the lid on tightly and shake the pan a little. After a minute or so, take off the lid and remove the open mussels to a large bowl and let cool. Discard any that won't open. When all the mussels are done, repeat with the clams. When all are cool, reserve some in their shells for serving, then take the remainder out of the shells and put in the mixing bowl.

Fish balls are kept in the refrigerator section of Asian stores. If unavailable, use extra shrimp.

Papaya grows everywhere in Thailand and is freely available. Young, unripened papaya is a basic salad ingredient in street food stalls, where it is pounded with fresh, spicy ingredients into a cold dish to accompany others. Now this staple dish has found great popularity in the West as the basis of a cold salad mixed with more expensive seafood such as crab, lobster, shrimp, or squid.

papaya salad with squid
som tam plamuk

1 lb. squid, cleaned, with tentacles separated

4 garlic cloves, peeled

3–4 small fresh red or green chiles

4 Chinese long beans, chopped into 2-inch lengths

1 lb. fresh green papaya, peeled, seeded, and cut into fine slivers

2 tomatoes, cut into wedges

¼ cup Thai fish sauce

2 tablespoons sugar

¼ cup lime juice

to serve

a selection of fresh firm green vegetables in season, such as iceberg lettuce, cucumber, or white cabbage

lime wedges

serves 4

To prepare the squid tubes, slit down both sides of the tubes and open out. Put on a board soft side up, then lightly run your knife diagonally, both ways, without cutting all the way through, making diamond patterns. The squid will then cook evenly and curl up attractively. Alternatively, just cut the tubes into slices.

Put 2¾ cups water in a saucepan, bring to a boil, add the squid, simmer for 3 minutes, drain, and set aside.

Using a large mortar and pestle, pound the garlic to a paste, then add the chiles and pound again. Add the long beans, breaking them up slightly. Stir in the papaya with a spoon. Lightly pound together, then stir in the tomatoes and lightly pound again. Add the squid and mix well.

Add the fish sauce, sugar, and lime juice, stirring well, then transfer to a serving dish. Serve with fresh raw vegetables and lime wedges, using any leaves as a scoop for the spicy mixture.

Note If Chinese long beans aren't available (though they are best for salads), use green beans—about 12, topped, tailed and halved.

Salads in general are perceived as lighter in the diet than other dishes. In Thailand, women regard this vermicelli salad as a slimming aid.

vermicelli salad

yam wun sen

4 oz. ground pork

10 raw shrimp, shelled, deveined, and coarsely chopped

½ package (4 oz.) thin rice vermicelli noodles

10 large dried black fungus mushrooms, soaked for about 10 minutes in cold water until soft, then coarsely chopped

1 large celery stalk, finely sliced

2 tablespoons Thai fish sauce

1 tablespoon sugar

3 tablespoons lime juice

¼ cup finely chopped small red chiles

¼ cup thinly sliced scallions, about 1 bunch

cilantro leaves, to serve

serves 4

Heat 3 tablespoons water in a saucepan, add the ground pork and shrimp, and stir well until the meat is just cooked through.

Add the noodles, mushrooms, celery, fish sauce, sugar, lime juice, chiles, and scallions.

Stir well, transfer to a serving platter, and top with cilantro leaves.

Notes Vermicelli are thin rice flour noodles. They are always sold dried, but are already cooked. Soak in cold water until soft, then chop coarsely.

If the dried black fungus mushrooms are very large, they may have a small hard piece in the middle, which should be cut out and discarded.

Traditionally, Asian diets did not make use of salads as we know them in the West. Over time, culinary arts and tastes have transferred across cultures, and Asian ingredients have fused with Western salad concepts. Here, we have a very Thai-style salad in a cold dish using traditional Thai ingredients. The result is a more flavorful cold salad dish than is normally seen on Western menus.

chicken salad with mint and roasted sesame seeds
yam gai

about 4 inches cucumber
2 skinless chicken breasts
3 small celery stalks, finely sliced
3 scallions, thickly sliced
2 tablespoons Thai fish sauce
2 tablespoons freshly squeezed lime juice
3 small red or green chiles, finely sliced
1 tablespoon finely chopped mint leaves
2 tablespoons roasted sesame seeds
2 tablespoons sesame oil

serves 4

To prepare the cucumber, cut it in half lengthwise and scrape out the seeds with a teaspoon. Cut in half crosswise, then cut each piece into matchsticks.

Bring a saucepan of water to a boil, add the chicken breasts, and poach at a gentle simmer until cooked through. Drain and let cool.

Shred the meat into small pieces over a bowl, letting any liquid it may retain fall into the bowl. Add the cucumber, celery, scallions, fish sauce, lime juice, chiles, mint, sesame seeds, and sesame oil and stir well. Spoon onto a plate and serve.

SNACKS AND ONE-DISH MEALS

Many Thai dishes are designed to be served with three or four others as part of a meal. Others were always single-serve dishes, such as this one, Pad Thai, which began as street food. The original recipe contained no meat but you can create your own flavor by adding your choice of meat or seafood. This has become the most-recognized Thai dish among foreigners.

3 tablespoons peanut or safflower oil

2 garlic cloves, finely chopped

2 tablespoons dried shrimp

4 oz. ready-fried tofu, cut into ½-inch cubes

2 large eggs

1 package (about 1 lb.) medium rice stick noodles

2 tablespoons preserved radish (chipo), finely chopped

4 scallions, finely sliced

¼ cup chopped roasted peanuts

1 cup (4 oz.) bean sprouts, rinsed, drained, and trimmed

1 teaspoon chile powder

1 tablespoon sugar

2 tablespoons Thai fish sauce

2 tablespoons light soy sauce

¼ cup freshly squeezed lemon or lime juice

a sprig of cilantro, coarsely chopped

1 lemon or lime, cut into wedges, to serve

serves 2–4

thai fried noodles
gueyteow pad thai

Heat the oil in a wok or skillet, add the garlic and dried shrimp, and sauté until golden brown. Add the ready-fried tofu and stir briefly. Break the eggs into the wok, cook for a moment, then stir. Add the noodles, stir well, then add the preserved radish and scallions. Add half the peanuts and half the bean sprouts. Stir well, then add the chile powder, sugar, fish sauce, soy sauce, and lemon juice.

Stir well and transfer to a plate. Top with the remaining peanuts and bean sprouts and the chopped cilantro. Serve with lemon wedges.

Notes Thai dishes are eaten with a fork and spoon, with the fork being used to push the food onto the spoon. The exceptions are noodle dishes, which were imported from China and so are eaten with chopsticks.

Sen lek or Jantaboon noodles are flat, medium rice flour noodles, often called rice sticks. They are usually dried. Soften them in a bowl of hot water from the tap for 10 minutes, then drain and rinse in cold water.

Traditional Thai meals are sharing occasions, with several dishes being prepared and presented, usually including a mix of something salty, something sweet, something crunchy and so on. This dish is seen as sweet. In the West, it has become a stand-alone snack dish. You need patience to prepare Mee Krop—it can take quite a while to get the optimum result, but it will be well worth your time.

crispy noodles
mee krop

peanut or safflower oil, for deep-frying

1 package (8 oz.) thin rice noodles

sauce

2 tablespoons peanut or safflower oil

4 oz. firm tofu, cut into ¼-inch cubes or thin strips

3 oz. dried shrimp

4 garlic cloves, finely chopped

4 pink Thai shallots or 2 regular ones, finely chopped

3 tablespoons Thai fish sauce

2 tablespoons palm sugar

2 tablespoons tomato sauce

¼ cup freshly squeezed lemon or lime juice (from 2 limes or 1½ lemons)

½ teaspoon chile powder

to serve

2 tablespoons peanut or safflower oil

1 egg, lightly beaten with 1 tablespoon cold water

¾ cup (3 oz.) bean sprouts, rinsed, drained, and trimmed

4 scallions, cut into 1-inch slivers

2 medium fresh red chiles, seeded and finely sliced lengthwise

2 whole heads of pickled garlic, finely sliced crosswise

serves 4

Fill a wok one-third full with the oil and heat until medium hot. Add the noodles and deep-fry until golden brown and crisp. Drain and set aside. Pour the oil into a heatproof container for another use.

Heat the 2 tablespoons oil for the sauce in the wok, add the strips of tofu, and sauté until crisp. Remove with a slotted spoon and set aside. Sauté the dried shrimp until crisp. Remove with a slotted spoon and set aside.

Add the garlic to the wok, sauté until golden brown, drain, and set aside. Add the shallots and sauté until brown. Add the fish sauce, sugar, tomato sauce, and lemon juice and stir well until the mixture begins to caramelize. Add the chile powder and the reserved tofu and garlic and stir until they have soaked up some of the liquid. Set aside.

Using a separate wok or skillet, heat the oil for the garnish and drip in the egg mixture to make little scraps of cooked egg. Drain and set aside. Return the main sauce to the heat and crumble in the crispy noodles, mixing gently and briefly. Transfer to a serving dish, sprinkle with bean sprouts, scallions, cooked egg scraps, chiles, and pickled garlic and serve.

Notes Sen mee are thin, dried rice flour noodles.

Pickled garlic is widely available in bottles or jars from Chinatown or Southeast Asian stores, or from mail order or online sources (page 142).

This quick vegetarian stir-fry *mélange* is widely popular because it offers something to suit almost any taste. The curry paste provides the hot flavor and the vegetables add a wholesome crispness. While the vegetable mixture shown here represents some popular ingredients, this recipe does lend itself to personal creativity, so add your favorite crunchy vegetables.

2 tablespoons peanut or safflower oil

2 garlic cloves, finely chopped

1 tablespoon Red Curry Paste (page 141)

1 lb. ready-cooked egg noodles

½ cup (3 oz.) coarsely sliced oyster mushrooms

2 small celery stalks, finely chopped

5–6 ears of baby corn, halved lengthwise

1 cup (4 oz.) bean sprouts, rinsed, drained, and trimmed

3 scallions, finely sliced diagonally

2 medium tomatoes, cut into wedges

3 tablespoons light soy sauce

1 teaspoon sugar

serves 4

egg noodles stir-fried with vegetables and curry paste
mee sua pad prik gaeng

Heat the oil in a wok until a light haze appears. Add the garlic, sauté for about 1 minute, then add the curry paste and continue stir-frying until the garlic is golden. Add the noodles, stir well, then add mushrooms, celery, corn, bean sprouts, scallions, tomatoes, soy sauce, and sugar, stirring quickly. Serve on a platter.

Note Ba me egg noodles are made from egg and wheat flour.

For most Thai, just hearing the name of this dish makes their mouths water. Usually eaten as a light lunch, it is also a favorite for a late supper. Surprisingly, it is not well known to foreigners, so if you visit Thailand, do try it at one of the all-night street food stalls.

mussel pancake

hoy tod

2 lb. mussels (about 30–40), soaked, cleaned, and debearded

2 tablespoons peanut or safflower oil, plus extra if necessary

1 large egg, beaten briefly with a fork

1 cup (4 oz.) bean sprouts, rinsed, drained, and trimmed

4 scallions, coarsely chopped

freshly ground white pepper, to taste

2 tablespoons light soy sauce

2 tablespoons Thai fish sauce

1 teaspoon sugar

a few fresh cilantro leaves, to serve

batter

3 tablespoons rice flour

3 tablespoons all-purpose flour

a pinch of salt

1 large egg

chile-vinegar sauce

¼ cup rice or white wine vinegar

2 small fresh chiles, finely sliced into rings

1 teaspoon sugar

serves 4

Heat a little water in a large saucepan, add the cleaned mussels, put the lid on tightly, and shake the pan until they open. Remove to a bowl as they do so, but discard any that won't open. Let the mussels cool a little, then remove them from their shells and discard the shells.

To make the chile-vinegar sauce, put the vinegar, sliced chiles, and sugar in a small bowl, mix well, and set aside.

To make the batter, mix the rice flour, all-purpose flour, and salt in a bowl. Make a hollow in the center, break in the egg, and add a splash of water. Whisk well, making sure there are no lumps—the mixture should have the consistency of thick cream.

Add the shelled mussels to the batter, stir to coat thoroughly, and set aside.

Heat the oil in a large wok or skillet, add the mussel and batter mixture, and tilt the pan from side to side to spread the mixture evenly over the surface. Cook the pancake for 1–2 minutes, then flip over and cook the other side briefly until it is set. Divide the pancake into 5–6 portions with a spatula and a wooden spoon. Lower the heat and pour the beaten egg into the pan. Quickly cook the pancake pieces in the egg, adding a little more oil if necessary.

Stir in the bean sprouts and scallions, then season with a sprinkling of white pepper. Add the soy sauce, fish sauce, and sugar, turning the pancake pieces over quickly to absorb the liquid. Transfer to a warm serving dish and top with fresh cilantro. Serve with the chile-vinegar sauce.

This recipe is very traditional in Thailand, particularly in busy lunchtime restaurants where workers pour in, demanding their meals quickly. The chicken and vegetables are cooked in advance in one big pot, and simmered slowly to keep warm. Then they can be served by pouring over rice or noodles as the customer orders. For parties, it means that you can prepare the chicken and vegetable component in advance too, then just keep it warm, ready to serve when guests want to eat—and you can escape from the kitchen, circulate, and enjoy your time with your guests.

chicken and vegetables on rice
khao nar gai

1 recipe Boiled Rice (page 11)

2 tablespoons peanut or safflower oil

2 garlic cloves, finely chopped

1 lb. boneless chicken breast or thigh, cut into 1-inch strips

3 oz. bamboo shoots, finely sliced

3 oz. canned straw mushrooms, whole or cut in half if large

about 5 ears of baby corn, halved lengthwise

½ small sweet red or green pepper, seeded and chopped

2 tablespoons Thai fish sauce

2 teaspoons sugar

1 teaspoon dark soy sauce

1 tablespoon cornstarch, mixed with ½ cup vegetable stock or cold water to make a thin paste

½ teaspoon freshly ground white pepper

4 scallions, sliced diagonally into 1 inch lengths

a few fresh cilantro leaves, chopped, to serve

serves 4

Put the cooked rice on a serving dish and keep it warm.

Heat the oil in a wok or skillet, add the garlic and sauté until golden brown. Add the chicken and stir-fry for a few seconds. Add the bamboo shoots, straw mushrooms, corn, and bell pepper and stir.

Stirring quickly after each addition, add the fish sauce, sugar, dark soy sauce, and 2 tablespoons water. Add more stock if the mixture becomes dry. Add the cornstarch mixture and stir until thoroughly blended to make a slightly thickened sauce, adding a little more water or flour/water mixture if necessary.

Add the white pepper and chopped scallions, stir quickly, then top with the coriander. Serve immediately over the cooked rice.

This traditional one-pot dish originates in the Muslim south of Thailand. There all the ingredients—chicken, rice, herbs, spices, and stock—are put in a large pot at the same time and cooked together. The flavors from the meat and other ingredients permeate the larger volume of rice, creating a delicious and flavorful dish. It makes an ideal one-pot meal to prepare at home.

curried rice with steamed chicken and fresh pickle

khao mok gai

3 tablespoons peanut or safflower oil

4 large garlic cloves, finely chopped

2½ cups fragrant Thai rice (jasmine rice), rinsed and drained

2 teaspoons curry powder

1 teaspoon salt

1 chicken, about 3 lb., cut up

2¾ cups chicken stock

fresh pickle

⅛ cup rice vinegar

3 teaspoons sugar

½ teaspoon salt

3-inch piece of cucumber

4 pink Thai shallots or 2 regular ones, finely chopped

2–3 small fresh red chiles, thinly sliced

an electric rice cooker or bamboo steamer

serves 4–6

Heat the oil in a wok or skillet, add the garlic, and sauté until golden brown. Stir in the rice, then add the curry powder and salt. Add the chicken pieces and stir well.

Either transfer the mixture to an electric rice cooker, add the stock, cover, and cook for 20 minutes, or put the mixture in a heatproof bowl, add the stock, and set in the top part of a steamer over boiling water and steam for 30 minutes. Turn off the heat and set aside with the lid on for about 30 minutes for the chicken to finish cooking.

While the chicken is steaming, make the pickle. Warm the vinegar, sugar, and salt in a small saucepan, stirring until the sugar has dissolved. Remove from the heat. Cut the cucumber in half lengthwise, scrape out the seeds with a teaspoon, then cut it in half again and slice very finely. Add to the sauce with the chopped shallots and chiles. Stir well, pour into a small bowl, and serve with the steamed chicken.

Laap is an original dish from Isaan, in the north-east of Thailand, where it will often be consumed with alcoholic drinks at social gatherings. As this is a less affluent region of Thailand, local people are creative in the meats they use for this style of cooking, often using beef, buffalo, river fish, shrimp, frogs, and other wild animals. The dish is hot and spicy, usually with a mixture of hot chile, garlic, and other ingredients that provide salty and sharp tastes.

spicy duck with sticky rice
khao neuw-laap pet

2½ cups sticky (glutinous) rice

1 tablespoon finely chopped lemongrass

1 tablespoon finely chopped galangal or ginger

3 tablespoons Thai fish sauce

3 tablespoons freshly squeezed lime juice, about 1½ limes

2 teaspoons sugar

1 teaspoon chile powder

4 skinless duck breasts, finely chopped

5 pink Thai shallots or 2 regular ones, thinly sliced

4 scallions, finely chopped

20 fresh mint leaves

raw crisp green vegetables, cut into bite-size pieces, to serve

serves 4

To make the sticky rice, put the rice in a bowl or pan, cover with water, and let soak for at least 3 hours, or overnight if possible. Drain and rinse thoroughly. Line the perforated part of a steamer with a double thickness of cheesecloth, and spread the rice over the cheesecloth. Heat the water in the bottom of the steamer to boiling and steam the rice over moderate heat for 30 minutes.

To make the spicy duck, put the lemongrass, galangal, fish sauce, lime juice, sugar, chile powder, and 2 tablespoons water in a saucepan and heat quickly. Add the duck and mix well until the meat is cooked through. Add the shallots and scallions and cook for a few seconds more. Then add fresh mint leaves, transfer to a serving dish, and serve with a selection of raw crisp green vegetables and steamed sticky rice.

Note Galangal is widely available in markets selling Southeast Asian produce. Fresh ginger is used as a common substitute in the West, though it has a totally different flavor and the recipe will not taste the same.

Khao and *pad* are perhaps the two most common and important words travelers in Thailand learn, because with these you can always get a basic yet filling dish in any restaurant. This is a staple recipe available all day in restaurants across the country. It is simple to prepare, not too hot to the taste and can be a light snack or a whole meal, depending on your portion size. While here we show only the most basic pork recipe, there are many variations found in restaurants, including versions made with chiles, seafood, or chicken.

1 recipe Boiled Rice (page 11)
2 tablespoons peanut or safflower oil
2 garlic cloves, finely chopped
1 lb. lean pork, such as fillet, finely slivered
2 large eggs
½ onion, coarsely sliced
½ cup (3 oz.) broccoli, cut into small florets
1 small carrot, thickly sliced
1 tablespoon dark soy sauce
1 medium tomato, cut into wedges
a pinch of sugar
2 tablespoons Thai fish sauce
2 scallions, finely sliced
freshly ground white pepper

serves 4

fried rice with pork and soy sauce
khao pad si-ew moo

First cook the rice according to the recipe on page 11. Let cool.

Heat the oil in a wok or skillet, add the garlic, and sauté until golden brown. Add the pork and stir-fry briefly over high heat. Break the eggs into the pan and stir well. Add the rice and mix well. Stir in the onion, broccoli, carrot, soy sauce, tomato, sugar, fish sauce, and scallions.

Transfer to a serving dish, season with white pepper, and serve.

This dish originated in China, but has been adapted to the Thai style with some local ingredients. Thailand has for centuries attracted migrants from neighboring countries, notably China, and each ethnic group has brought diversity to the Thai culinary repertoire. This dish is based on pork grilled in traditional Chinese style, as found in Chinese restaurants worldwide—served with rice or noodles, in soups, and as a filling in buns. Here it has a Thai flavor.

grilled pork with rice
khao moo daeng

2 lb. boneless spareribs
¼ cup tomato purée
2 tablespoons dark soy sauce
¼ cup light soy sauce
¼ cup sugar

chile and vinegar sauce
¼ cup rice vinegar
2 small fresh red chiles, cut into thin rounds

salty sauce
2 cups pork or chicken stock
2 tablespoons light soy sauce
3 tablespoons sugar
2 tablespoons Thai fish sauce
2 teaspoons rice flour mixed with 1 tablespoon water

to serve
½ cucumber, about 8 inches, thinly sliced
4 scallions, cut into 1-inch lengths
a few fresh cilantro leaves, coarsely chopped
2–4 hard-cooked eggs, shelled and quartered

serves 4

To prepare the pork for the grill, put the tomato purée, dark and light soy sauces, and sugar in a large bowl. Add the pork strips and stir well to coat evenly in the sauce. Let marinate for 1 hour.

Preheat a broiler or grill. Put the marinated pork under or over the heat, turning the pieces from time to time until cooked through.

While the pork is cooking, make the sauces. To make the chile and vinegar sauce, mix the vinegar and chile in a small bowl and set aside.

To make the salty sauce, heat the stock in a saucepan, add the soy sauce, sugar, and fish sauce, and stir well. Bring to a boil and simmer for 1 minute. Sprinkle the rice flour mixture over the liquid and whisk gently until the sauce thickens.

Cut the pork into very thin slices. Put a heap of rice on each plate and top with thin slices of grilled pork. Pour over a generous helping of the salty sauce. Add sliced cucumber, some scallion, cilantro, and hard-cooked egg to each plate and serve with the chile and vinegar sauce.

This recipe is a light, easy-to-make, quick-fry dry noodle dish. In my early schooldays, this was one of my regular lunchtime meals—it provided enough nutrition to get me through the afternoon, but could be eaten quickly enough to leave most of the lunch break free to kick a soccer ball around the school yard.

river noodles with beef and dark soy sauce
pad si yew nua

2 tablespoons peanut or safflower oil

4 garlic cloves, finely chopped

1 lb. lean beef, such as fillet, finely sliced

2 large eggs

1 package (1 lb.) wide rice noodles

1 teaspoon finely sliced fresh ginger

1 cup (8 oz.) broccoli, thickly sliced

2 tablespoons dark soy sauce

1 teaspoon sugar

3 tablespoons Thai fish sauce

freshly ground white pepper

1 green chile, finely shredded

serves 4

Heat the oil in a wok, add the garlic, and sauté until golden brown. Add the beef, stir, then cook briefly. Break the eggs into the mixture, stir, add the noodles and ginger, cook quickly, then add the broccoli and stir again.

Add the dark soy, sugar, and fish sauce, stirring quickly after each addition. Stir again, transfer to a serving dish, sprinkle with white pepper, top with the shredded chile, then serve.

Notes To make the beef easier to slice, wrap it in plastic wrap and freeze for 1 hour. Unwrap and slice very finely.

Sen yai are broad, flat, rice flour noodles. If using fresh noodles, soak in hot water to separate, then boil for 1 minute. If using dried noodles, soak in a bowl of boiling water for 4 minutes, then boil for 2–3 minutes.

CURRIES AND PICKLES

Salty eggs are a favorite in Thailand. Traditionally, we prefer duck eggs, because they are considered firmer when hard-cooked. If you can't find duck eggs, use large chicken eggs instead. The eggs can be eaten simply on their own, or served with rice, salad, or crunchy Chinese long beans. To make the salty eggs, you have to start three weeks ahead, but if you have access to a good Asian market, you should be able to buy them already prepared.

spicy long beans with salty eggs
pad prik king kai-kem

peanut or safflower oil, for deep-frying, plus 2 tablespoons extra

8 oz. ready-fried tofu, finely sliced

2 teaspoons finely chopped garlic

1 tablespoon Red Curry Paste (page 141)

1½ cups (8 oz.) Chinese long beans, chopped into 1 inch lengths

2 tablespoons light soy sauce

¼ cup vegetable stock

1 teaspoon sugar

1 tablespoon ground roasted peanuts

4 kaffir lime leaves, finely chopped

salty eggs

8 eggs (duck eggs are preferred, but large chicken eggs are quite satisfactory)

1 cup salt

serves 4

To prepare the salty eggs, put the eggs in a preserving jar, being careful not to crack the shells. Put the salt and 3 cups water in a saucepan and heat until the salt has dissolved. Let cool, then pour the mixture over the eggs in the jar. Seal the jar and leave for 3 weeks, after which the eggs can be boiled or fried. To use them in this dish, you will need 2 hard-cooked eggs (see note). Cut the eggs in half with the shells still on, then scoop out the halves with a teaspoon. Cut each half in half again and set aside.

Fill a wok one-third full with the peanut oil and heat until a piece of noodle will fluff up immediately. Add the tofu and deep-fry until the white sides are golden brown. Remove with a slotted spoon, drain, and set aside.

Heat the 2 tablespoons of oil in a wok or skillet, add the garlic, and sauté until golden brown. Stir in the red curry paste. Add the long beans, soy sauce, stock, sugar, peanuts, lime leaves, and fried tofu. Stir-fry until the beans are done to your taste (I like them very crisp). Serve on a platter with the salty eggs.

Notes Though you could make this dish with regular green beans, Chinese long beans are very good in cold or cool dishes. They have more bite and crunch than regular beans. Find them in Chinese and Southeast Asian markets and sometimes in larger supermarkets.

For hard-cooked salty eggs, boil 5–6 minutes for hen eggs or 6–8 minutes for duck eggs. Alternatively, put the eggs in cold water, bring to a boil, turn off the heat, and let cool.

Curry originated in the Indian subcontinent and migrated eastwards long before it traveled west to Europe and North America. Over centuries, it has been adapted to local ingredients and tastes in several other Asian countries, notably Thailand, where it is generally considered that many of our curries are even hotter and more flavorful than their Indian cousins. Red curry paste is used as the core curry ingredient in many Thai dishes.

vegetable curry
gaeng ped pak

2 tablespoons peanut or safflower oil

2 tablespoons Red Curry Paste (page 141)

2¾ cups coconut cream

2¾ cups vegetable stock

4 Chinese long beans, cut into 1-inch pieces

4 carrots, cut into matchsticks

5 ears of baby corn, cut into 1 inch pieces

½ cup (3 oz.) cauliflower, cut into florets

4 kaffir lime leaves, coarsely chopped

2 large fresh red or green chiles, coarsely sliced

3 tablespoons light soy sauce

2 teaspoons sugar

½ teaspoon salt

6 small round green eggplant, quartered

30 fresh basil leaves

serves 4

Put the oil in a saucepan, heat well, then quickly stir in the curry paste. Add the coconut cream, mixing well. Add the vegetable stock and stir briefly.

Add the long beans, carrots, corn, cauliflower, lime leaves, chiles, soy sauce, sugar, salt, and eggplant. Stir well, then cook for a few minutes until the vegetables are cooked to your taste (I like them crisp but tender).

Add the basil leaves, stir once, then ladle into a bowl and serve with other Thai curries and rice.

Green curry is my mother's speciality, so this is a staple dish from my childhood. With more than 20 years' experience in the food industry and being a head chef myself, I can confidently say that I have never tasted a green curry as good as my mother's.

green curry with shrimp

gaeng keow-wan gung

2 tablespoons peanut or safflower oil

2 garlic cloves, finely chopped

2 tablespoons Green Curry Paste (page 141)

12 raw jumbo shrimp, shelled and deveined

2¾ cups coconut cream

2¾ cups vegetable stock

2 large fresh red chiles, sliced diagonally into thin ovals

¼ cup Thai fish sauce

8 round green Thai eggplant, quartered, or 1 Chinese eggplant, cut into ½-inch slices

1 tablespoon sugar

30 fresh sweet basil leaves

serves 4

Heat the oil in a large saucepan, add the garlic, and sauté until golden brown. Stir in the curry paste, mixing well. Add the shrimp and stir-fry until just cooked through. Add the coconut cream and bring to a boil, stirring constantly. Add the stock. Return to a boil, stirring constantly.

Keeping the curry simmering, add the chiles, fish sauce, eggplant, and sugar and simmer until the eggplant are cooked but still crunchy (do not overcook or the shrimp will be tough).

Stir in the basil leaves just before pouring into the serving bowl. Serve with rice and other Thai dishes.

In this quick, pan-fried curry, the flavor comes mainly from chile oil. As soon as the pan and oil are heated, add the clams, steam for just a few minutes, and they're cooked.

baby clams with chile oil and holy basil

hoy pad nam prik pow

1 tablespoon peanut or safflower oil

2 garlic cloves, finely chopped

1 tablespoon chile oil (see below)

2 lb. baby clams, in the shell

2 tablespoons Thai fish sauce

2 small red chiles, finely sliced

20 leaves holy basil

chile oil (nam prik pow)

2 tablespoons peanut or safflower oil

¼ cup finely chopped garlic

¼ cup finely chopped shallots

¼ cup finely chopped dried red chiles

½ teaspoon salt

1 tablespoon sugar

serves 4

To make the chile oil, heat the oil in a wok, add the garlic, and stir-fry until golden brown. Remove the garlic with a fine sieve and set aside. Add the shallots to the wok and stir-fry until brown and crispy. Remove with a sieve and set aside. Add the chiles to the wok and stir-fry until they begin to darken. Remove with a sieve.

Using a mortar and pestle, pound the chiles, garlic, and shallots together. Put the mixture back in the wok and stir over low heat. Stir in the salt and sugar and mix to make a thick, slightly oily reddish-black sauce, not a paste. Use 1 tablespoon for this recipe and reserve the rest for another use.

To cook the clams, heat the oil in a large skillet, add the garlic, and sauté until golden brown. Add the 1 tablespoon chile oil and the baby clams and stir thoroughly. Add the fish sauce, chiles, and ¼ cup water. Stir thoroughly, add the basil, cover the pan, and let steam for a few minutes until the clams have opened. Discard any that don't open. Stir again, transfer to a warmed dish, and serve.

Paenang curries differ from most other Thai dishes in being rather dry—normally, they are very wet, with accompanying sauces similar to some Indian curries. While it is not clear how this curry entered our cuisine, it is thought, judging from the name, that it may have originated in the far south of Thailand, near Malaysia (Penang is in Malaysia).

chicken panaeng curry

panaeng gai

2¾ cups coconut cream

2 tablespoons peanut or safflower oil

2 garlic cloves, finely chopped

2 tablespoons Panaeng Curry Paste (page 141)

1 lb. boneless chicken breast, thinly sliced

3 tablespoons Thai fish sauce

2 teaspoons sugar

4 kaffir lime leaves, finely chopped

20 holy basil leaves

2 long red chiles, slivered

serves 4

Gently heat the coconut cream in a small saucepan, but do not let it boil. Set aside. Reserve 1 tablespoon for serving.

Heat the oil in a wok or skillet until a light haze appears, add the garlic, and sauté until golden brown. Add the curry paste and stir-fry for a few seconds. Add the chicken and stir-fry until it is lightly cooked. Add the coconut cream, stir well, then add the fish sauce and sugar and stir well.

Just before serving, stir in the lime leaves, holy basil, and some of the slivered chiles. Spoon into a bowl and top with the reserved 1 tablespoon coconut cream and the remaining chiles.

A real fusion of Chinese (noodles) and Indian (curry), prepared in a particularly Thai way, this dish adds to the variety and excitement of Thai cuisine. It could well originate further south, around the Straits of Malacca, where the Nonya peoples, a mixture of Chinese and Malay, developed many dishes that crossed the boundaries between Chinese and Muslim culinary styles.

chicken curry noodle
gueyteow gaeng

½ package (8 oz.) dried medium rice noodles

1 lb. boneless chicken, cut into 1-inch cubes

2 hard-cooked eggs

2 tablespoons peanut or safflower oil

1 block prepared fried tofu, finely sliced

4 pink Thai shallots or 2 regular ones, finely sliced

4 garlic cloves, finely chopped

1 tablespoon Red Curry Paste (page 141)

2¾ cups coconut cream

1 teaspoon curry powder

¼ cup Thai fish sauce

2 teaspoons sugar

2 tablespoons ground roasted peanuts

cilantro leaves, to serve

serves 4

Soak, rinse, and drain the noodles. Put the chicken in a small saucepan and cover with water. Simmer gently for 10–15 minutes, then remove from the heat and set aside, reserving the cooking water. Cut the hard-cooked eggs into quarters and set aside.

Heat the oil in a wok or skillet, add the sliced tofu, and sauté until slightly crisp. Drain and set aside. Reheat the oil and sauté the shallots until dark golden brown and crisp. Transfer to a plate. Add the garlic to the skillet and sauté for a few seconds until golden brown. Stir in the curry paste and cook for a few seconds. Add the coconut cream, stir thoroughly, and heat through for another few seconds.

Using a slotted spoon or strainer, remove the chicken from its saucepan and add to the mixture. Stir to make sure each piece is covered with the curry. Add 2 cups of the water in which the chicken has been cooked (make up the amount with cold water if necessary), then add the curry powder, fish sauce, and sugar. Stir well and cook for about 5 minutes.

Have serving bowls ready. Bring a saucepan of water to a boil, put the noodles in strainer with a handle, and dip into the water for 2–3 seconds to warm through. Drain and divide between the serving bowls. Arrange the quartered egg on top of the noodles. Add the ground peanuts to the chicken curry soup, stir, and pour over the noodles. Top with the fried tofu, fried shallots with a little of their oil, then the cilantro.

Note Sen lek or Jantaboon noodles are flat, medium rice flour noodles, often called rice sticks. They are usually dried. Soften them in a bowl of hot water for 10 minutes, then drain and rinse in cold water.

The long white radish—mooli or daikon—is popular in Chinese cooking, but has also been adopted extensively in Thailand, especially in its preserved form. It particularly helps in recipes where you want a salty taste with a crunchy texture. You can buy preserved radish in Asian markets, but if you would like to try preserving them yourself, it is very easy.

pork with fried preserved radish
pad chipo

2 tablespoons peanut or safflower oil

2 teaspoons finely chopped garlic

8 oz. loin of pork, finely sliced

2 large eggs

2–3 oz. preserved radish (store-bought or homemade—see note), sliced diagonally ⅛-inch thick

3 medium scallions, finely chopped into rings

2 tablespoons light soy sauce

2 tablespoons Thai fish sauce

1 teaspoon sugar

½ teaspoon freshly ground white pepper

cilantro leaves, to serve

preserved white radish (chipo)

1 lb. white radish, peeled and cut in half lengthwise, then into matchsticks

1¼ cups sugar

1 cup rice vinegar

2 tablespoons salt

serves 4

If you are making your own preserved white radish, put the pieces of radish in a bowl, sprinkle with salt, and leave overnight. Next day, rinse the pieces thoroughly at least twice in cold water.

Arrange the pieces of radish in a preserving jar and set aside. Put the sugar and vinegar in a saucepan and bring to a boil. Remove from the heat and let cool. When cold, pour the mixture over the radish. Close the jar firmly and leave for 1 week.

After 1 week, remove the radish and spread on a rack to dry in the open air. In Thailand we leave them to sun-dry, which takes about 24 hours.

To make the fried pork, heat the oil in a wok, add the garlic, and sauté until golden brown. Add the pork, stir, and cook until the meat is slightly opaque. Break the eggs into the wok, spreading the broken yolks a little. Before the egg sets, add the preserved radish and scallion and stir rapidly. Add the soy sauce, fish sauce, sugar, and white pepper, still stirring rapidly. Transfer to a platter, top with cilantro leaves, and serve.

Note There are two kinds of preserved radish—sweet or salty. The one used in this recipe is the sweet kind. If you have the salty kind, soak in cold water for 5–10 minutes, then drain and squeeze out the water before proceeding with the recipe.

In the north of Thailand, they have adapted the traditional curry taste to get a sweet and sour flavor, common to other non-curry Thai dishes. This is achieved by using pickled garlic to provide a blend of sweet and sour tastes. In the north, this dish would be eaten with plain sticky rice.

pork curry with pickled garlic
gaeng hung lay

2 tablespoons peanut or safflower oil

2 garlic cloves, finely chopped

2 tablespoons Red Curry Paste (page 141)

1 lb. boneless pork with a little fat, finely slivered

2¾ cups coconut cream

2 inches fresh ginger, peeled and finely chopped

⅓ cup chicken stock or water

3 tablespoons Thai fish sauce

2 teaspoons sugar

½ teaspoon ground turmeric

2 teaspoons freshly squeezed lemon or lime juice

4 whole heads of pickled garlic, finely sliced crosswise

serves 4

Heat the oil in a wok or skillet, add the garlic, and sauté until golden brown. Add the curry paste and stir well. Add the pork and stir-fry over high heat until cooked through, approximately 5 minutes.

Pour in the coconut cream and stir until the liquid begins to reduce and thicken. Do not boil. Add the ginger, chicken stock, fish sauce, sugar, turmeric, lemon juice, and pickled garlic, stirring constantly.

Transfer to a large bowl and serve.

Note Pickled garlic is widely available in bottles or jars from Chinatown or Southeast Asian stores, or from mail order or online sources (page 142).

If you like a milder curry, this is the dish for you. It originates in the Muslim south of Thailand, where people prefer less spicy foods in general. It also shows an Indian influence in the use of potatoes and nuts as key ingredients. While lamb is not part of the traditional Thai diet, this dish could be made with either lamb or chicken if you prefer.

massaman beef curry
massaman nua

2¾ cups coconut cream

2 tablespoons peanut or safflower oil

2 garlic cloves, finely chopped

2 tablespoons Massaman Curry Paste (page 141)

1 lb. lean beef, cut into 1-inch cubes

3 tablespoons freshly squeezed lemon or lime juice

2 teaspoons sugar

3 tablespoons Thai fish sauce

2¾ cups beef stock or water

4 small potatoes, quartered

3 tablespoons whole roasted peanuts

4 pink Thai shallots or 2 regular ones, quartered

sprigs of cilantro, to serve

serves 4

Gently warm the coconut cream in a small saucepan until it just starts to separate. Remove from the heat and set aside.

Heat the oil in a wok or skillet, add the garlic, and sauté until golden brown. Add the curry paste, mix well, and cook for a few seconds. Add half the warmed coconut cream and cook for 2–3 seconds, stirring all the time, until the mixture bubbles and starts to reduce.

Add the beef and stir it into the sauce to make sure that each piece is thoroughly coated. Stirring after each addition, add the lemon juice, sugar, fish sauce, stock, and the remainder of the warmed coconut cream. Simmer gently for 15 minutes, stirring from time to time.

Add the quartered potatoes and simmer for a further 5 minutes. Add the peanuts and cook for 5 minutes more. Stir in the shallots and cook for 5 more minutes, then pour into a serving dish and top with fresh cilantro. Serve with fragrant Thai rice (jasmine rice) and other dishes, such as a soup, a stir-fry, a spicy salad, and fresh pickle (page 72).

I developed this modern Thai recipe to meet the growing demand for dishes that combine the best of culinary cultures across the region. Like so many Thai, my family has a mixed heritage of Chinese and Thai, so some of our recipes have developed to reflect this combination. In Southeast Asia, all noodle recipes are of Chinese origin and so are usually eaten with chopsticks.

stir-fried beef noodles with curry paste
ba mee pad prik gaeng

2 tablespoons peanut or safflower oil

4 small garlic cloves, finely chopped

1 tablespoon Green Curry Paste (page 141)

1 lb. beef, thinly sliced

4 nests of egg noodles

1 tablespoon dark soy sauce

3 tablespoons Thai fish sauce

2 teaspoons sugar

1 cup (4 oz.) bean sprouts, rinsed, drained, and trimmed

½ cup (4 oz.) broccoli, cut into small pieces, about 1 inch

1 carrot, cut into fine matchsticks

cilantro leaves, to serve

serves 4

Heat the oil in a wok or skillet, add the garlic, and stir-fry until golden brown. Add the curry paste and stir well.

Stirring once after each addition, add the beef, drained noodles, soy sauce, fish sauce, sugar, bean sprouts, broccoli, and carrot.

Mix well, transfer to a serving bowl or plate, and top with torn cilantro.

Note Ba mee are egg and wheat flour noodles, and always sold fresh. Rinse them in warm water, boil for 3–4 minutes, then drain.

MAIN DISHES

Ever popular in my own restaurants, this is a dish I can always recommend to people new to the tastes of Thai food. They enjoy the combination of fresh shrimp with the strongly aromatic flavor of basil. It's easy to vary the amount of chile too, in case very spicy food isn't to your taste. This is an excellent dish for the beginner cook.

shrimp with chile and basil
kung pad prik krapow

2 tablespoons peanut or safflower oil

2 garlic cloves, finely chopped

2 small fresh red or green chiles, finely chopped

12 raw jumbo shrimp, shelled and deveined, tail on

2 medium onions, halved and thickly sliced

3 tablespoons Thai fish sauce

2 tablespoons light soy sauce

1 teaspoon sugar

30 fresh holy basil leaves

serves 4

Heat the oil in a wok or skillet, add the garlic and chiles, and stir-fry until the garlic begins to brown. Stir in the shrimp, then add the onions, fish sauce, soy sauce, sugar, and basil, mixing well. Cook until the shrimp are cooked through (it will take just a few minutes—they will become opaque). Transfer to a dish and serve with other Thai dishes, including rice.

Variations *Pad prik krapow* means "stir-fried with basil and chile." You can vary this dish and, instead of shrimp, use 1 lb. of pork, beef, or chicken, all finely chopped or ground. In Thailand, the shrimp would also be chopped or ground, but in the West, whole shrimp are used instead.

The sweet and sour topping from this dish can be adapted to suit vegetarians. Instead of fish sauce, use extra soy sauce, then serve with rice and other vegetarian dishes.

sweet and sour fish

pad preow wan pla

1 sea bass, about 1 lb.

peanut or safflower oil, for frying

sweet and sour topping

2 teaspoons cornstarch

2 tablespoons peanut or safflower oil

2 garlic cloves, finely chopped

½ cup (4 oz.) pineapple chunks, fresh or canned

about 3 inches cucumber, quartered lengthwise, then thickly sliced crosswise

1 small onion, halved, then sliced into thin segments

2 small tomatoes, quartered

3 medium scallions, coarsely chopped into 1-inch lengths

2 large fresh red chiles, sliced diagonally

2 tablespoons Thai fish sauce

1 tablespoon light soy sauce

1 teaspoon sugar

½ teaspoon freshly ground white pepper

electric deep-fryer (optional)

serves 4

Make a diagonal cut in each side of the fish.

Fill a wok or deep-fryer one-third full with the oil or to the manufacturer's recommended level. Heat until a scrap of noodle will puff up immediately.

Add the fish and fry until golden and crispy. Remove from the oil, drain, and put on a serving dish.

Mix the cornstarch with ⅓ cup water in a small cup and set aside.

Heat the oil in a wok or skillet, add the garlic, and stir-fry until golden brown. Stirring constantly, add the pineapple, cucumber, onion, tomatoes, scallions, chiles, fish sauce, soy sauce, sugar, and pepper.

Stir the cornstarch mixture to loosen it, then add to the vegetables and stir briefly to thicken the sauce. Pour over the fish, then serve.

Though the pineapple is a Thai addition, this simple chicken stir-fry originated in China. Thai pineapples are wonderfully sweet, and the sweet-and-spicy combination is typical in Southeast Asian cuisines.

chicken stir-fried with ginger and pineapple
gai pad king sapparot

6 large dried Chinese black fungus mushrooms

2 tablespoons peanut or safflower oil

2 garlic cloves, finely chopped

8 oz. boneless chicken, finely sliced

1 cup (8 oz.) pineapple chunks, fresh or canned

2 inches fresh ginger, peeled and cut into fine matchsticks

2 tablespoons light soy sauce

2 tablespoons Thai fish sauce

4 scallions, chopped into 1-inch pieces

2 long fresh red chiles, cut diagonally into fine ovals

1 teaspoon sugar

freshly ground black pepper, to taste

serves 4

Soak the mushrooms in cold water for 10 minutes, then drain and set aside. If large, cut them into smaller pieces, discarding any hard parts.

Heat the oil in a wok or skillet, add the garlic, and stir-fry until golden brown. Add the chicken and stir well. Stirring constantly, add the mushrooms, pineapple, ginger, soy sauce, fish sauce, scallions, chiles, sugar, and pepper. As soon as the pepper is stirred in, transfer to a dish and serve.

This dish is a combination of Thai and Chinese cuisines. Duck is not a traditional ingredient in Thai cooking, so when it does appear it is often cooked using roast duck prepared in the Chinese style. For this recipe, the key ingredient is the tamarind water. Prepare it as described on page 49.

duck with tamarind sauce
ped makham

4 duck breasts, with or without skin

3 tablespoons Thai fish sauce

2 large red chiles, cut into small strips

cilantro leaves, to serve

duck marinade

4 garlic cloves, finely chopped

1 tablespoon finely chopped cilantro root

1 teaspoon ground cumin

2 tablespoons Thai fish sauce

1 tablespoon light soy sauce

2 teaspoons sugar

tamarind sauce

2 tablespoons peanut or safflower oil

2 large garlic cloves, finely chopped

1 tablespoon grated fresh ginger

2 tablespoons tamarind water (page 49)

2 tablespoons vegetable stock or water

2 tablespoons sugar

serves 4

To make the marinade, put the garlic, cilantro root, cumin, fish sauce, soy sauce, and sugar in a bowl and mix well. Add the duck, coating it well with the mixture, and leave to marinate for 1 hour.

When ready to cook, remove the duck from the marinade and pat it dry with paper towels. Preheat the broiler to high heat and cook the duck for 5 minutes on each side, then slice diagonally and set aside.

To make the tamarind sauce, heat the oil in a wok or skillet, add the garlic, and stir-fry until golden. Add the ginger, tamarind water, stock, and sugar, stirring well. Add the sliced duck and sprinkle with fish sauce and strips of chile, stirring well.

Transfer to a serving dish, top with cilantro leaves, and serve.

Common in farming areas, this recipe comes from the north, where whole families work in the fields from dawn to dusk. The wife will prepare the dish and take it to the fields, where it will be eaten with sticky rice—often cold—for lunch and throughout the day. Back at home in the evening, if there is some left over, it will be served for dinner too. You can also serve this as a sauce with raw or blanched vegetables, crispy pork crackling (see note below), or shrimp crackers.

pork and chile sauce

nam prik ong

2 tablespoons peanut or safflower oil

3 garlic cloves, finely chopped

1 tablespoon Red Curry Paste (page 141)

8 oz. ground pork

2 large tomatoes, finely chopped

2 tablespoons Thai fish sauce

2 tablespoons freshly squeezed lemon or lime juice

1 teaspoon sugar

to serve (optional)

shrimp crackers

Thai pork crackling

salad leaves

sliced shallots or other vegetables

steamed rice

serves 4

Heat the oil in a wok or skillet until a light haze appears. Add the garlic and sauté until golden brown. Stir in the curry paste and cook briefly.

Add the pork and stir-fry until the meat loses its pinkness. Add the tomatoes, stir, cook for 5 seconds, then add the fish sauce, lemon juice and sugar. Stir-fry for 2 minutes until the flavors are thoroughly blended.

Serve in a small bowl with your choice of shrimp crackers, Thai pork crackling, salad leaves or other vegetables, or rice.

Note Thai pork crackling can be found in Asian stores. Chinese markets might call it by its Cantonese name *ji pay*, while in Mandarin it is known as *zhu pi*.

An easy dish to prepare and cook, this is a suitable recipe for those new to Thai cooking. The combination of garlic and chile ensures a very hot and traditional Thai flavor.

pork with garlic and fresh chile
moo tod kratiam prik sod

2 tablespoons peanut or safflower oil

3 large garlic cloves, finely chopped

1 lb. lean pork, finely sliced

2 tablespoons Thai fish sauce

2 tablespoons light soy sauce

2 large fresh red chiles, finely sliced

serves 4

Heat the oil in a wok or skillet until a light haze appears. Add the garlic and stir-fry until golden brown. Add the pork and stir-fry briefly.

Add the fish sauce, soy sauce, and chiles, stirring briefly all the time. By now the pork should be cooked through. Spoon onto a serving dish and top with sliced scallions. Serve with 3–4 other Thai dishes, including rice, noodles, and perhaps fresh pickle.

Variations Instead of the pork, use a similar quantity of finely sliced chicken or beef, or shelled and deveined shrimp.

Shrimp or squid with garlic and peppercorns is another favorite Thai dish, both in Thailand and in Thai restaurants worldwide. Follow the main recipe, but instead of the chiles, use 1 teaspoon white peppercorns, crushed with a mortar and pestle.

My Aunt Chinda is a wonderful Thai cook in her own right. She greatly influenced me, both in the actual cooking of traditional Thai food, and subsequently in the business of running and managing restaurants, because she has owned and run restaurants in several of the major cities of Thailand. This recipe is one of her favorites.

stir-fried beef with eggplant and bean sauce
nua pad makua tow jiew

2 tablespoons peanut or safflower oil

2 garlic cloves, finely chopped

4 small fresh red or green chiles, finely chopped

8 oz. boneless tender beef, sliced into thin slivers

1 long Thai eggplant (like Chinese or Japanese), thickly sliced, or 1 long green eggplant, thickly sliced

2 tablespoons bean sauce, yellow or black

1 tablespoon light soy sauce

1 teaspoon sugar

20 sweet basil leaves

steamed rice, to serve

serves 4

Heat the oil in a wok or skillet, add the garlic, and stir-fry until golden brown. Add the chiles and stir well. Add the beef, stir, then add the eggplant. Stir again, add the bean sauce, soy sauce, and sugar, then stir-fry until the eggplant is just cooked through (cover with a lid—the steam will help it cook faster).

Add the basil leaves, stir thoroughly, then spoon onto a dish and serve with steamed rice.

Agriculture is Thailand's main industry. The farmers prepare a day's food in the morning to take into the fields for lunch and snacks. Their diets are very simple, usually quite high in carbohydrates rather than protein, as energy is the key to a hard day's work. This recipe is found mainly in the Central Regions. When serving it in the West, it should be served not just with rice, but with three to four other dishes.

fish and spicy sauce

nam prik pla yang

1 mackerel

1 medium onion, finely chopped

5 garlic cloves, peeled

4 large fresh red chiles, coarsely chopped

3 tablespoons Thai fish sauce

3 tablespoons lemon or lime juice

1 tablespoon cilantro leaves, finely chopped

to serve

your choice of salads, lettuce, sliced radishes, celery, carrot and cucumber

aluminum foil

serves 4

Wrap the fish in foil leaving the top open and set it under a preheated broiler until thoroughly cooked through. Remove to a plate and let cool. When cool, break up the fish with your fingers to make small pieces. Discard any bones and set the flesh aside.

Wrap the onion, garlic, and chiles in foil, again leaving the top open, and set them under the broiler. Cook until they begin to soften.

Using a large mortar and pestle, pound the onion, garlic, and chiles to form a liquid paste. Stir in the fish sauce and lemon juice, then fold in the fish (see note). Spoon into a small bowl and sprinkle with cilantro. Serve surrounded by a selection of salads, crisp lettuce, radish, celery, carrot, and cucumber.

Note In Thailand, the fish would be mashed to a paste before folding into the mixture.

SWEET THINGS

Thailand is a country that is rich in fruits and vegetables, and they are generally of high quality, as demonstrated by the volume of exports to other nations. Fruit is not just served at the end of a meal—it also appears in main meals, especially in spicy curries, stir-fries, dips, and salads. In curries, you find pineapples and lychees. Salads are made with rose apples, guavas, pomelos, green mangoes, or green papaya. Mangoes are also used in spicy dips and lychees as a filling in deep-fried spring rolls. A popular street food snack is green fruit sprinkled with salt and chile. You can also blend any combination of tropical fruits into a colorful and juicy salad that will sparkle like a bowl of gems on the table.

thai fruit salad

1 small ripe papaya

½ pineapple

1 ripe mango

4 rose apples (optional) or regular apples

1 ripe guava

1 tablespoon freshly squeezed lemon or lime juice

1 tablespoon sugar

10 mint leaves, finely chopped, to serve

serves 4

Peel, halve, and seed the papaya. Cut the flesh into small cubes.

Peel, core, and cube the pineapple.

Cut the cheeks off the mango, cut the flesh in diamond shapes down to the skin, turn the cheeks inside out, then scoop off the pieces with a fork.

To prepare the rose apples, cut them in half, cut out the cores, and cut the flesh into small cubes.

Cut the guava in half, scoop out and discard the seeds, then cut the flesh into small cubes.

Arrange the fruit in a bowl. Add the lemon juice, sugar, and chopped mint. Mix well and chill in the refrigerator before serving.

While all Thai fruits are suitable for making mouth-watering and cleansing sorbets, perhaps the star in our collection is lychee sorbet. If you cannot find fresh lychees in your neighborhood (they are best in fall), this recipe is also good with canned lychees.

lychee sorbet

¾ cup sugar

1 lb. fresh lychees, peeled, seeded and finely chopped, or about 14 oz. canned lychees, drained and chopped

a few fresh lychees, to serve (optional)

an electric ice cream maker (optional)

serves 4

To make a sugar syrup, put the sugar in a saucepan with 1¼ cups water. Bring to a boil and stir until the sugar dissolves. Let cool.

Put the lychees in a blender, add the cooled syrup, and blend until smooth. Freeze for about 1 hour until the mixture is slushy and frozen around the edges. Remove from the freezer, transfer to the blender, blend again, then return the mixture to the freezer for about 30 minutes.

Alternatively, if you have an electric ice cream maker, churn until the mixture is completely frozen. Transfer to a freezerproof container and freeze until ready to serve.

Before serving, let soften in the refrigerator for about 20 minutes, then serve in scoops with a few fresh lychees, if available.

Notes This recipe is suitable for many fruits. In particular, try papaya, pineapple, kiwifruit, and mango.

Make extra sugar syrup, then decant into a storage bottle and keep in the refrigerator for use in drinks and desserts. It is a very useful ingredient.

Everywhere in Thailand, the most common flavoring used in ice cream manufacture is coconut. Though other fruits may be favored in local areas, nationally it is the coconut that wins. It offers a rich, fresh taste and is normally creamy white in color. Sometimes coconut is mixed with other fruits such as lotus seeds, jackfruit, or other locally available varieties. Here we have a basic ice cream recipe.

coconut ice cream

2¾ cups coconut milk

1¼ cups heavy cream

¾ cup sugar

2 large eggs

3 tablespoons shredded coconut, lightly toasted in a dry skillet

a small loaf pan or similar freezer-proof container

an electric ice cream maker (optional)

serves 4

Put the coconut milk, cream, and sugar in saucepan and bring to a boil. Remove from the heat.

Put the eggs in a bowl and beat well. Gradually beat the boiled coconut milk mixture into the eggs, then let cool completely and chill.

When cold, pour the mixture into a small loaf pan, cover, and freeze until firm. Chop up the ice cream, then beat until smooth, using an electric mixer or food processor. Spoon the mixture back into the loaf pan, cover, and freeze for several hours until firm.

Alternatively, if you have an electric ice cream maker, churn until the mixture is completely frozen. Transfer to a freezerproof container and freeze until ready to serve.

Serve sprinkled with the toasted coconut.

Sticky rice with mango is probably Thailand's favorite sweet dish. Many will even ask if it is available on a menu before ordering their entrées. I am biased in my belief that Thai native mangoes are the softest and sweetest available and it is their texture that makes this dish such a delight. Outside Thailand, we make do with mangoes from other sources. Often, the best available are from India or Pakistan—better than the larger ones from South America or the Caribbean. Remember that sticky rice must be soaked for at least 3 hours or overnight, before steaming for 30 minutes or so.

sticky rice with mango
khao niew mamuang

2 cups sticky (glutinous) rice

1¼ cups coconut milk

2 tablespoons sugar

½ teaspoon salt

4 ripe mangoes

2 tablespoons coconut cream, to serve

serves 4

Soak and cook the sticky rice (page 11) and use while still warm.

Put the coconut milk and sugar in a small saucepan and heat gently, stirring all the time, until the sugar has dissolved. Do not let boil.

Stir in the salt and the warm sticky rice and set aside.

To prepare the mangoes, cut the 2 cheeks off each one, as close to the pit as possible. Cut each cheek into 4–6 long wedges, cutting through the flesh but not through the skin. Peel back and discard the skin. (The flesh around the pit is the cook's treat!)

Pile a mound of sticky rice in the center of a serving dish and arrange the slices of mango around it. Pour the coconut cream over the rice and serve warm or cold. Alternatively, serve the rice in small bowls, add a few slices of mango, then trickle the coconut cream over the top.

Thai desserts in general can be time-consuming to prepare. While other recipes might be more popular within Thailand, for Thai living abroad, this recipe offers a time-saving treat, with ingredients commonly available. If you are new to Thai cuisine, this will be a quick and easy starting point in preparing Thai sweet dishes. Palm sugar, produced from the sap of the coconut palm, has a deep caramel flavor. It is sold in cans or compressed cakes—it should be soft brown, with a distinctive toffee-like aroma. The cakes will keep well in a sealed jar. You will find palm sugar in Asian stores or by mail order (page 142).

sweet potatoes with palm sugar and coconut milk

man gaeng buad

1 lb. sweet potatoes, peeled and coarsely cut 1-inch cubes

1 teaspoon salt

2¾ cups coconut cream

⅓ cup palm sugar

serves 4

Put the sweet potato cubes in a bowl of cold water, add the salt, and let soak for 30 minutes. Drain.

Heat the coconut cream in a saucepan, add the sweet potato cubes, and bring to a boil. Add the palm sugar and stir until it dissolves. Stir in 1¼ cups water. Return to a boil and simmer until the sweet potato is tender. Remove from the heat and serve warm.

Sago pearls are one of the most surprising and delicious additions to a sweet dish you can think of. Sago is made from the heart of the sago palm, while tapioca is made from the root of a tropical plant called cassava or manioc. You will find both items sold under both names in Asian stores—either will do. Often, it is only the size of the pearl which is different. In this dish, they are used in a cold refreshing pudding served with crushed ice which brings out the scent of the melon and coconut milk. Sweet and revitalizing.

melon and coconut milk with sago
sa-koo taeng

½ cup sago

1¾ cups coconut milk

⅓ cup sugar

1 ripe melon, preferably cantaloupe, cut into ½-inch cubes

crushed ice (optional)

serves 4

Wash the sago in cold water and drain.

Pour 2¾ cups water into a saucepan and bring to a boil. Add the sago and return to a boil. When the sago floats to the surface (at least 15 minutes), it is cooked. Remove with a slotted spoon as it rises and transfer to a bowl of cold water.

When all the sago has been transferred, remove from the cold water and drain. Spoon into a serving bowl and set aside.

Heat the coconut milk in a saucepan. Stir in the sugar and 2¾ cups water, bring gently to a boil, then remove from the heat and let cool.

When cool, pour into a bowl, add the sago and melon, and serve with crushed ice. If you do not have crushed ice, chill the mixture in the refrigerator before serving.

If the body could survive on fruit alone, then maybe Thailand would be the best country for fruit lovers to live. Fruits grow in abundance all year and are of excellent quality, freshness, and value. Some of the fruits are very specific to regions and may not even make it to the markets of Bangkok. A great variety of these fruits are used in drinks, including bananas, guavas, papaya, oranges, pineapples, watermelon, coconuts, longans, pomelos, rambutans, and mangoes. You can try this recipe with any of these fruit, and also with temperate zone fruit such as apples and pears.

tropical fruit drinks
nam-pun

1 ripe pineapple, peeled, cored, and cut into small slices

ice cubes

sugar syrup (page 126)

a pinch of salt

a blender

Serves 1

Put a few slices of pineapple in a blender with ice cubes, syrup, and a pinch of salt to taste (salt will bring out the flavor of the fruit). Blend well, then pour into glasses.

The variations shown here are made with papaya and guavas.

thai tea

nam cha

Tea originated in China and moved through to Thailand over the centuries, brought by Chinese immigrants. Now many varieties are grown in the cooler, wetter hill districts of northern Thailand, which have the most suitable climate for tea. Thailand consumes many varieties of tea, and in many formats, from traditional Chinese tea, drunk plain and without sugar, to the ice tea popular in other countries, and the English style with milk and sugar. Whatever your taste in tea, you should find a variety you will like here.

Thai leaf tea
sugar, to taste
ice
sweetened condensed milk

Hot tea Cha ron
Brew a pot of Thai tea and serve to your taste.

Ice tea without milk *Cha dum yen*
Brew a pot of Thai tea, add sugar to taste, and stir well. Let cool to room temperature, then pour over a full glass of ice.

Ice tea with milk *Cha yen*
Brew a pot of very strong hot tea. For each person, add 1 teaspoon sweetened condensed milk and sugar to taste. Let cool, then serve with a full glass of ice.

thai coffee

ka fae

Coffee, like tea, is being grown now in the Hill Tribes' areas of the north, in a project sponsored by King Rama IX. It is encouraged as an alternative to opium (banned as a cash crop in Thailand), but which is a centuries-old traditional crop of the Hill Tribes of Thailand, Burma, and neighboring countries. In the future, perhaps Thai coffee will find a niche in world markets, but in the meantime, readers may like to sample local coffee when traveling in Thailand.

freshly ground coffee, Thai if possible
sugar, to taste
ice
sweetened condensed milk
unsweetened condensed milk

Hot coffee *Ka fae ron*
Brew a pot of filtered coffee, using your favorite blend or authentic Thai coffee if available.

Sweet ice black coffee *Oliang*
Brew strong black coffee, add sugar to taste, and stir well. Let cool, then serve over ice.

Ice coffee with milk *Ka fae yen*
Brew strong black coffee, then for each person add 1 teaspoon sweetened condensed milk and sugar to taste. Stir well. Let cool to room temperature and pour the coffee over a full glass of ice. Top with unsweetened condensed milk.

curry pastes

When making curry pastes, the quantities needed to make a single curry are too small to make properly. I have developed these recipes in larger, easy-to-make quantities. I have suggested the amount you should need for each recipe in the ingredients list for that recipe. However, you can adjust the amounts used to suit your own taste.

green curry paste

kruang gaeng keow-wan

1 teaspoon coriander seeds

1 teaspoon cumin seeds

1 teaspoon white peppercorns

1 tablespoon chopped fresh lemongrass

1 inch fresh galangal or ginger, peeled and chopped*

2 long green chiles, chopped

10 small green chiles, chopped

2 tablespoons chopped garlic

3 pink Thai shallots or 1 regular, chopped

3 cilantro roots, chopped

1 teaspoon chopped kaffir lime skin, or finely chopped lime leaves

2 teaspoons shrimp paste

Using a mortar and pestle, grind all the ingredients to a thick paste.

panaeng curry paste

kruang gaeng panaeng

10 long dried red chiles, seeded and chopped

5 pink Thai shallots or 2 regular ones, chopped

2 tablespoons chopped garlic

2 stalks of lemongrass, chopped

1 inch fresh galangal, peeled and chopped

1 teaspoon ground coriander

1 teaspoon ground cumin

3 cilantro roots, chopped

1 teaspoon shrimp paste

2 tablespoons roasted peanuts

Using a mortar and pestle, grind all the ingredients into a paste.

Note The recipes make about ½–¾ cup paste. If necessary, spoon the remainder into ice cube trays, freeze, then keep in labeled plastic bags for future use. One cube yields about 1 tablespoon paste. In the West, ginger is often substituted for galangal, though it has a different flavour.

red curry paste

kruang gaeng daeng

8 long red dried chiles, seeded and chopped

1 teaspoon ground coriander seed

½ teaspoon ground cumin seed

1 teaspoon freshly ground white pepper

2 tablespoons chopped garlic

2 stalks of lemongrass, chopped

3 cilantro roots, chopped

1 teaspoon chopped kaffir lime skin, or finely chopped lime leaves

1 inch fresh galangal or ginger, peeled and chopped

2 teaspoons shrimp paste

1 teaspoon salt

Using a mortar and pestle, grind all the ingredients into a paste.

massaman curry paste

kruang gaeng massaman

10 long dried red chiles, seeded and chopped

1 tablespoon ground coriander seeds

1 teaspoon ground cinnamon

1 teaspoon ground cumin seeds

1 teaspoon ground cloves

2 whole star anise

1 teaspoon ground cardamom

1 teaspoon freshly ground white pepper

6 pink Thai shallots or 3 regular, chopped

7 garlic cloves, chopped

2 inches fresh lemongrass, chopped

½ inch fresh galangal, peeled and chopped

1 tablespoon chopped kaffir lime skin or finely chopped lime leaves

1 tablespoon shrimp paste

1 tablespoon salt

Using a mortar and pestle, grind the dried spices. Add the remaining ingredients, blending after each addition, to form a paste.

websites, asian markets, and mail order

THAI INGREDIENTS

Bangkok Center Grocery
104 Mosco Street
(between Mott and Mulberry)
New York, NY 10013
Tel: 212-349-1979
www.thai-grocery.com
*Ingredients, cookware, herbs
and spices, frozen and prepared
Thai foods, and Thai beer. Store
is open daily 10 am to 8 pm,
personal shoppers only. Online
from www.thai-grocery.com.*

Bangkok Market
4757 Melrose Avenue
Los Angeles, CA 90029
Tel: 323-662-9705
www.bangkokmarket.com
*Wide range of ingredients,
including fresh, at this LA store.
Online store sells Thai cookware
and ingredients.*

GourmetSleuth.com
PO Box 508
Los Gatos, CA 95030
Tel: 408-354-8281
Fax: 408-395-8279
www.GourmetSleuth.com
*A source of cookware from
around the world, with a section
on Asian cookware.*

ImportFood.com
PO Box 2054
Issaquah, WA 98027
Tel: Mon-Fri toll free
888-618-THAI (8424)
or 425-687-1708
Fax: 425-687-8413
http://ImportFood.com
*Online Thai supermarket selling
cookware and ingredients. Fresh
ingredients include herbs and
galangal.*

pacificrim-gourmet.com
i-Clipse Inc.
4905 Morena Boulevard,
Suite 1313,
San Diego, CA 92117
Tel: 1-800-910-WOKS
(continental USA)
or 858-274-9013
Fax: 1-858-274-9018
http://pacificrim-gourmet.com
*Extensive range of Asian and
Mexican cookware and
ingredients.*

quickspice.com
Tel: 323-728-4762
Fax: 323-888-0780
www.quickspice.com
*California-based mail order
company. Try them for Asian
cookware, tableware, and
ingredients.*

Temple of Thai
PO Box 112
Carroll, IA 51401
Tel: 877-811-8773
Fax: 712-792-0698
www.templeofthai.com
*Thai ingredients and fresh
produce including galangal.
Thai cookware, such as sticky
rice steamers, granite mortars
and pestles, and cast iron pans.*

The Wok Shop
718 Grant Avenue
San Francisco, CA 94108
Tel: 1-415-989-3797
or 888-780-7171
www.wokshop.com
*Asian cookware, including Thai
sticky rice steamers and serving
baskets.*

THAI HERBS AND OTHER PLANTS

Evergreen YH Enterprises
PO Box 17538
Anaheim, CA 92817
Tel/Fax: 714-637-5769
http://www.evergreenseeds.com
*More than 300 varieties of Asian
vegetable and herb seeds,
including Thai basils, and Thai
round and long green eggplant.*

Four Winds Growers
www.fourwindsgrowers.com
*To grow your own kaffir lime
trees, see this brand in person
at California retail nurseries and
garden centers, or order online.*

Thai Herbs & Spices
PO Box 151835
Austin, TX 78715-1835
Tel: 512-280-9130
www.thaiherbs.com
*Thai herbs available in 4–6 inch
pots. Not available in winter
(December to March). Payment
by check, money order, or
Paypal. A wide and interesting
range.*

COCKTAIL CRAB CLAWS

Gorton's Fresh Seafood
128 Rogers Street
Gloucester, MA 01930
Tel: 800-335-3674
www.gortonsfreshseafood.com
*Cocktail claws and other
seafood online.*

conversion charts

Weights and measures have been rounded
up or down slightly to make measuring
easier.

Volume equivalents:

American	Metric	Imperial
1 teaspoon	5 ml	
1 tablespoon	15 ml	
¼ cup	60 ml	2 fl.oz.
⅓ cup	75 ml	2½ fl.oz.
½ cup	125 ml	4 fl.oz.
⅔ cup	150 ml	5 fl.oz. (¼ pint)
¾ cup	175 ml	6 fl.oz.
1 cup	250 ml	8 fl.oz.

Weight equivalents: / Measurements:

Imperial	Metric	Inches	Cm
1 oz.	25 g	¼ inch	5 mm
2 oz.	50 g	½ inch	1 cm
3 oz.	75 g	¾ inch	1.5 cm
4 oz.	125 g	1 inch	2.5 cm
5 oz.	150 g	2 inches	5 cm
6 oz.	175 g	3 inches	7 cm
7 oz.	200 g	4 inches	10 cm
8 oz. (½ lb.)	250 g	5 inches	12 cm
9 oz.	275 g	6 inches	15 cm
10 oz.	300 g	7 inches	18 cm
11 oz.	325 g	8 inches	20 cm
12 oz.	375 g	9 inches	23 cm
13 oz.	400 g	10 inches	25 cm
14 oz.	425 g	11 inches	28 cm
15 oz.	475 g	12 inches	30 cm
16 oz. (1 lb.)	500 g		
2 lb.	1 kg		

Oven temperatures:

110°C	(225°F)	Gas ¼
120°C	(250°F)	Gas ½
140°C	(275°F)	Gas 1
150°C	(300°F)	Gas 2
160°C	(325°F)	Gas 3
180°C	(350°F)	Gas 4
190°C	(375°F)	Gas 5
200°C	(400°F)	Gas 6
220°C	(425°F)	Gas 7
230°C	(450°F)	Gas 8
240°C	(475°F)	Gas 9

index

143